Will it Microwave?

Will it Microwave?

Joan Hood

Front cover photography by David Burch

Illustrations by Jane Brewster

The author and publisher would
like to thank Sanyo for the loan of their microwave
model EMP710N for food testing.

Published in 1986 by
The Hamlyn Publishing Group Limited,
Bridge House, 69 London Road,
Twickenham, Middlesex, England.

Second impression 1987

ISBN 0 600 32665 9

Set in Monophoto Plantin 113 and Univers 685
by Tameside Filmsetting Limited, Ashton-under-Lyne, Lancashire

Printed in Hong Kong

CONTENTS

USEFUL FACTS AND FIGURES

Notes on metrication

In this book quantities are given in metric and Imperial measures. Exact conversion from Imperial to metric measures does not usually give very convenient working quantities and so the metric measures have been rounded off into units of 25 grams. The table below shows the recommended equivalents.

Ounces	Approx g to nearest whole figure	Recommended conversion to nearest unit of 25	Ounces	Approx g to nearest whole figure	Recommended conversion to nearest unit of 25
1	28	25	11	312	300
2	57	50	12	340	350
3	85	75	13	368	375
4	113	100	14	396	375
5	142	150	15	425	425
6	170	175	16 (1 lb)	454	450
7	198	200	17	482	475
8	227	225	18	510	500
9	255	250	19	539	550
10	283	275	20 (1¼ lb)	567	575

Note: When converting quantities over 20 oz first add the appropriate figures in the centre column, then adjust to the nearest unit of 25. As a general guide, 1 kg (1000 g) equals 2.2 lb or about 2 lb 3 oz. This method of conversion gives good results in nearly all cases, although in certain pastry and cake recipes a more accurate conversion is necessary to produce a balanced recipe.

Liquid measures The millilitre has been used in this book and the following table gives a few examples.

Imperial	Approx ml to nearest whole figure	Recommended ml	Imperial	Approx ml to nearest whole figure	Recommended ml
¼ pint	142	150 ml	1 pint	567	600 ml
½ pint	283	300 ml	1½ pints	851	900 ml
¾ pint	425	450 ml	1¾ pints	992	1000 ml (1 litre)

Spoon measures All spoon measures given in this book are level unless otherwise stated.

Can sizes At present, cans are marked with the exact (usually to the nearest whole number) metric equivalent of the Imperial weight of the contents, so we have followed this practice when giving can sizes.

Notes for American and Australian users
In America the 8 fl oz measuring cup is used. In Australia metric measures are now used in conjunction with the standard 250-ml measuring cup. The Imperial pint, used in Britain and Australia, is 20 fl oz, while the American pint is 16 fl oz. It is important to remember that the Australian tablespoon differs from both the British and American tablespoons; the table below gives a comparison. The British standard tablespoon, which has been used throughout this book, holds 17.7 ml, the American 14.2 ml, and the Australian 20 ml. A teaspoon holds approximately 5 ml in all three countries.

British	American	Australian
1 teaspoon	1 teaspoon	1 teaspoon
1 tablespoon	1 tablespoon	1 tablespoon
2 tablespoon	3 tablespoon	2 tablespoons
$3\frac{1}{2}$ tablespoons	4 tablespoons	3 tablespoons
4 tablespoons	5 tablespoons	$3\frac{1}{2}$ tablespoons

An Imperial/American to solid and liquid measures

Imperial	American	Imperial	American
Solid measures		Liquid measures	
1 lb butter or		$\frac{1}{4}$ pint liquid	$\frac{2}{3}$ cup liquid
margarine	2 cups	$\frac{1}{2}$ pint	$1\frac{1}{4}$ cups
1 lb flour	4 cups	$\frac{3}{4}$ pint	2 cups
	1 pint	$2\frac{1}{2}$ cups	1 lb granulated
or castor sugar	2 cups	$1\frac{1}{2}$ pints	$3\frac{3}{4}$ cups
1 lb icing sugar	3 cups	2 pints	5 cups ($2\frac{1}{2}$ pints)
8 oz rice	1 cup		

Note: When making any of the recipes in this book, only follow one set of measures as they are not interchangeable.

Food was tested in 600 and 650 watt ovens with a turntable. If your oven has a different output cooking times will need to be adjusted accordingly. If your oven does not have a turntable you may need to turn and rotate some dishes by hand.

INTRODUCTION

Many people find the microwave has transformed their lives, enabling them to cook at speed with the chore of washing-up cut to a minimum. Others, frustrated by a series of failures, have settled for using their microwaves for thawing and reheating only. I suspect that this is because their expectations were too high. They probably thought the microwave could do all that a conventional cooker could do, only faster.

But microwaving isn't just fast cooking. It is a different cooking concept and as such takes time and practice to master. The first thing to understand is that it is a moist form of cooking. When used for foods that are traditionally boiled, steamed or poached, it is highly successful. When it comes to 'baking' and 'roasting' – terms which are not really applicable to microwave cooking – the results are quite different and often disappointing.

So which foods should you be cooking in the microwave?

In the A–Z section of this book you will find instructions for cooking a whole range of foods. As well as explaining how to prepare and cook them, I have tried to describe how they look and taste in comparison with the same foods cooked conventionally. With some foods the microwave produces superior results: fish, vegetables and fruit are particularly successful. For other foods – bread and biscuits or cookies among them – a conventional cooker does a better job. And for the perfect roast I think you need to combine microwaving with conventional cooking.

You may or may not agree with my conclusions when you cook the foods yourself, but at least you will know what to expect before you start.

CHOOSING A COOKER

When choosing a microwave, you have to decide – apart from the obvious question of how much money you are prepared to spend – on the degree of sophistication you feel you need.

The microwave market can be divided into three categories: basic cookers, multi-featured cookers and combination cookers.

The basic cooker has an output of between 450 and 600 watts and two power levels: full and defrost (or low). In some models there is a turntable.

In the range of multi-featured cookers you can expect to find one or more of the following refinements.

• VARIABLE POWER •

This allows you to choose the speed at which you cook by using a wide range of power levels. There is no uniform way of describing the power levels. On some microwaves the levels are simply numbered; on others they are described as high, medium, defrost and low, while some use such cooking terms as simmer, braise or roast. For this reason the term 'full power' is used throughout this book to indicate the highest setting of the oven.

• TEMPERATURE PROBE •

This is a built-in device which enables you to cook by temperature and is particularly useful for meat cookery. In some models you monitor the temperature yourself, in others the microwave switches off automatically when the required temperature is reached.

• SENSOR CONTROL •

Models with this facility sense the food temperature and switch off automatically when the food is cooked.

• MEMORY •

This enables you to pre-programme the microwave so that it can cook in your absence. Some models can store a favourite recipe and carry out the cooking with a simple touch on the controls.

• SHELVES •

A few microwaves incorporate a shelf enabling you to cook on two levels. Although this means you can cook more food at a time, it takes longer for it to cook because of the increased quantity and the food must be carefully arranged for best cooking results.

• BROWNING ELEMENT •

Some models have a built-in browning element like a grill (broiler), but you may consider your conventional grill (broiler) is adequate for your needs.

Finally there are the combination cookers which will give you the best of both worlds. In one unit you have microwaving for speed and conventional – usually fan-assisted – cooking for colouring and crisping.

When you have decided which category appeals to you, collect the brochures, watch as many demonstrations as you can and ask questions. To a great extent your choice must depend on the amount and kind of cooking you intend doing in your microwave.

If you want it for thawing, reheating and occasional cooking, a basic model will be adequate. If you need a cooker that can tell you when the food is cooked or be pre-programmed to cook in your absence, then you will need one of the more sophisticated models. But don't be tempted by one of the more advanced models unless you *are* going to make use of its special features, because they are obviously more expensive.

If you have a conventional cooker, a combination cooker would be something of a luxury but it could be a good choice if you were starting from scratch or changing a conventional cooker and have only limited space for appliances.

COOKING UTENSILS

Don't feel that you have to rush out and buy new equipment just because you cannot use metal saucepans and baking trays or sheets in the microwave. If you look in your kitchen cupboards, you will find a wide choice of suitable containers that are in everyday use.

• GLASS •

A whole range of ovenproof glass – jugs (pitchers), bowls and dishes, together with glass ceramics, provided that there is no metal trim – is ideal for use in the microwave and will withstand the high temperatures reached when cooking foods with a high fat and sugar content.

Don't use lead crystal glasses but ordinary table glasses can be used for warming drinks. It is wiser not to use such glass for long-term cooking because although the microwaves will not damage it, the very hot food might.

• CHINA •

Provided they do not have a metallic trim, china plates, dishes, cups and jugs can be used. Vegetables can be cooked and served in their own dishes, which not only saves on washing-up but keeps the vegetables hotter. White ovenproof porcelain is useful and the simple, elegant lines of this range make particularly attractive serving dishes.

Don't use cups or jugs with glued-on handles as the glue could melt!

• PLASTIC •

There is an enormous range of plastic containers available. As a rough guide if a container is dishwasher-proof, it will probably be suitable for short-term cooking and heating in the microwave, but not for cooking foods with a high fat or sugar content that are likely to reach high temperatures. You should not use melamine as it is likely to scorch, nor yogurt or ice cream cartons as they are apt to buckle.

• POTTERY •

This should be fully glazed. Unglazed pottery is porous and absorbs some of the microwave energy, which slows down the cooking and makes the containers hot.

• WOOD AND WICKER •

Wooden boards and bowls can be used for heating bread and rolls but, as they contain natural moisture, prolonged heating will cause them to dry out and they will eventually crack. The same applies to wicker baskets. Use them for short-term heating provided neither glue nor metal staples have been used in their construction.

• TESTING CONTAINERS •

If you are uncertain as to the suitability of a container for use in the microwave, here is the way to test it.

Place the container in the cooker together with a glass half full of water. Microwave on full power for 1 minute. If the water is warm and the dish cool, it can be used. If the dish is warm, it can still be used but cooking in it will take longer. If the dish is hot and the water cool, it should not be used as the dish has been absorbing microwave energy.

Glass and plastic containers can be tested in the same way but need only 15 seconds on full power.

• SHAPE •

The shape of the container plays an important part in achieving good results. A straight-sided shallow container is better than a deep dish as the heat will spread more evenly. Best of all is the ring shape because microwaves have access to all sides of the food and there is no slow-to-cook centre. Round containers are also good because of the equal access of microwaves to all sides; the centre, however, will cook more slowly.

With square and rectangular shapes microwaves have double

access at the corners and this is where overcooking can occur. Shielding the ends half-way through the cooking can help to eliminate this problem and allow the centre, which always cooks more slowly, to catch up.

• SPECIAL RANGES •

As you find yourself making more and more use of the microwave, you may well decide that some of the specially designed containers would be useful and you will find plenty to choose from.

Freezer owners looking for alternatives to foil dishes are well catered for in the range of freezer-to-microwave ovenware. The containers are manufactured from high density polythene and can be used over and over again. Designs include ring moulds, pudding basins or bowls, pie or flan and ramekin dishes (custard cups).

Ovenboard ovenware offers more scope as it can be used in a conventional oven up to 200C, 400F, gas 6 as well as in the microwave and freezer. Available in this range are casserole and pudding dishes, trays and a divided meal plate. They can be carefully washed and re-used sometimes, though they are designed as disposable.

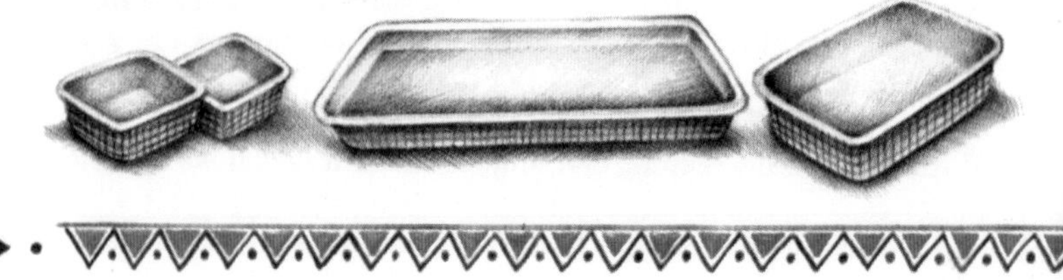

ACCESSORIES

When it comes to accessories for the microwave you will find plenty of temptations. How many you actually need depends on the sort of cooking you will be doing.

A browning dish will help to colour and crisp food though you may be perfectly happy to do this in your conventional grill or frying pan (broiler or skillet).

If you choose to cook large pieces of meat and poultry regularly, then a roasting rack is more satisfactory to use than fiddling about with upturned saucers. It will also double as a bacon rack.

A special microwave thermometer will take some of the guesswork out of cooking meat and, unlike ordinary food thermometers, it can be left in the microwave whilst the meat is cooking.

A really large jug (pitcher) is essential for making sauces and custards so the liquids can rise without boiling over. Just right for the job is a 2-litre/3½-pint/9-cup polypropylene one through which you can watch the liquid rising during cooking. Its squat round shape makes it ideal, too, for such things as steamed sponge and suet puddings.

If you regularly reheat plates of food, a microwave plate cover could be a good investment. It has a stepped rim, so it fits most sizes of plates, and an adjustable vent to allow steam to escape. It would presumably work over round shallow dishes, too, and reduce your expenditure on other covering materials.

Apart from greaseproof (waxed) and absorbent kitchen paper you will need a bumper-size roll of cling film (plastic wrap) for covering foods.

A selection of boiling and roasting bags is useful for the clean and quick cooking of vegetables and meat. Remember to use an elastic band and *not* a metal tie to fasten them.

A supply of wooden cocktail sticks (toothpicks) for anchoring foil, skewering small pieces of meat and piercing food; a packet of elastic bands and you'll be well equipped.

WHAT ARE MICROWAVES?

Before you start to cook, do read through your handbook as well as these pages. You will get much better results if you understand not only how the microwave works but why you apply certain techniques when cooking in it.

What are microwaves? They are a form of electromagnetic energy in the same category as radio and television waves. As their name – micro – implies they are short waves, less than 12.5 cm/5 in long, and are a source of energy, not heat. They are non-ionising, which means they do not build up in the body or change the cell structure, so are not dangerous.

With their special characteristics they are reflected off metal, pass through certain materials like glass, china and paper and are absorbed and utilised by food and liquid.

When you switch on your microwave, the electricity supply is converted by a magnetron in the cooker into microwaves. A wave guide then directs the microwaves into the cooker cavity and they then bounce off the metal walls, pass through the container and into the food, hitting it from all angles. This isn't quite as haphazard as it sounds because a fan diffuses the energy so that it enters the food as evenly as possible. In some cookers a turntable assists this further by revolving the food through the wave patterns.

As the microwaves pass through the air in the cooker, no heat is generated, so the cooker stays cool but, as soon as they penetrate the food, they set the water molecules in it jumping around at billions of times a second. All this friction creates tremendous heat and the heat cooks the food – fast.

Because these microwaves only penetrate food to a depth of 3.5–5 cm/1½–2 in, the food beyond this point is heated by conduction. The period of standing, which you will find recommended in many recipes, allows the generated heat to spread evenly through the food and complete the cooking.

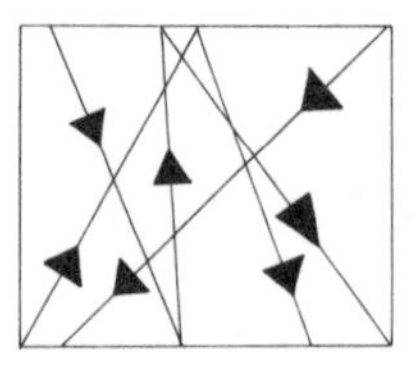

Left: microwaves bounce off the metal walls.

Right: microwaves penetrate food to a depth of 3.5–5 cm/1½–2 in.

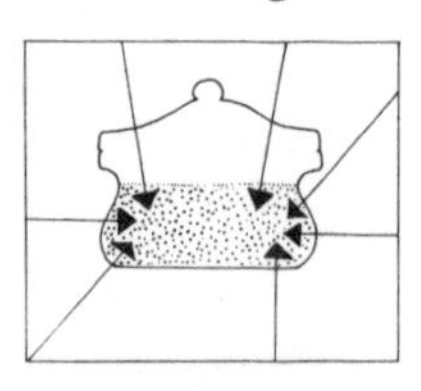

COOKING TECHNIQUES

Whichever way you choose to cook food, timing is important; in microwaving, because it is so fast, it is critical. Overcooking by only seconds can often make the food at best unpalatable and at worst inedible. Timing is affected by a number of factors.

As in conventional cooking, there are a number of basic techniques you need to learn and apply to get the best results from your microwave.

• SHAPE •

The shape of the food affects the way it cooks. A neat, compact shape will cook evenly and easily. An irregular shape will need care and attention to ensure that the heat gets evenly distributed through both the thin and thick areas.

• DENSITY •

This affects the rate at which the heat moves to the centre of the food. Meat, with its dense texture, takes longer to cook than a cake with a light open texture.

• QUANTITY •

The more you put into the microwave, the longer it will take to cook. This is because whatever quantity of food you put in the cooker, the amount of available energy remains the same and has to be shared around.

• TEMPERATURE •

The colder the food, the longer it will take to cook. Food taken straight from the refrigerator will need longer than food at room temperature.

You can see from the above how difficult it is to give exact timings. Not only does the food have many variables but individual cookers vary too. That's why you should always cook for the shortest recommended time, or even less; check the food and return it, if necessary, for further cooking. Undercooking can be remedied, overcooking can't.

• ARRANGING •

As the outer areas of any food receive the most microwave energy, the thickest and densest pieces should be arranged round the edges with the thinner or more delicate foods in the centre.

Individual items like jacket potatoes or ramekin dishes (custard cups) should be arranged in a ring shape with a space left in the middle.

• REARRANGING •

To ensure that all the food receives an equal amount of exposure to the microwave energy, it is re-positioned during cooking. This means that food cooking quickly on the outer edge is slowed down by being moved to the centre and vice versa. In this way heating is equalised and the food is cooked evenly.

• TURNING •

Large pieces of meat and poultry are turned over once or twice during their cooking period to ensure even cooking.

When the food itself cannot be turned, as in the case of puddings and cakes, the dish is turned. If your cooker has a turntable, you will probably not need to do this.

• STIRRING •

This is the way to turn or rearrange such foods as custards, sauces or scrambled eggs. You simply stir the outer edges, as they start to cook, into the centre mixing them in with the uncooked parts and distributing the heat throughout the whole. Small amounts of vegetables and mince or ground beef should also be stirred. You will only need to stir any food once or twice during a short cooking cycle.

• SHIELDING •

This is the way to protect certain areas – the thin end of a piece of meat, the tail end of a fish or the wing tips of a chicken – from overcooking. Small pieces of foil are wrapped round or secured with a wooden cocktail stick (toothpick) to any parts that appear to be overcooking and may burn.

• PIERCING •

Foods with a skin or membrane – jacket potatoes, tomatoes or egg yolks, for example – need to be pierced before cooking. If this is not done, the build-up of steam eventually bursts through the skin and spatters the food.

• STANDING •

Because food continues to cook for a short time after removal from the microwave, it is important to give it a standing time, so that the heat generated can continue to spread through the food and complete the cooking. This is particularly important with large pieces of meat and poultry. If the food was microwaved until the heat had fully penetrated the centre, the outside would be overcooked.

• COVERING •

Foods that need to be kept moist during cooking should be covered. This means cooking in a roasting or boiling bag or in a dish covered with a lid, a plate or cling film (plastic wrap). The cling film (plastic wrap) should be vented by piercing it with the point of a knife or turning back one edge to allow the steam to escape. When removing cling film (plastic wrap) always lift it up from the side farthest away from you so that the steam is directed away from your face.

Foods that need to be dry, like bread and cake, should not be covered except when they are being reheated. They can then be stood on, or wrapped in, absorbent kitchen paper to prevent them becoming soggy.

Another reason for covering foods is to contain any spattering and keep the oven clean. Any foods that have a tendency to spit or pop like bacon and baked beans should be covered with a piece of absorbent kitchen paper.

REHEATING

By far the best and safest way to reheat food is in a microwave. The conventional method with its attendant health risks invariably produces dried-out food that looks and tastes unappetising. In a microwave food is reheated so quickly that germs have no time to breed while the piping hot food looks and tastes freshly cooked.

For even heating spread the food out in a shallow dish whenever possible. Stir the food or turn the dish at least once to distribute the heat.

Sliced meat is best reheated with a covering of gravy or a sauce so that it does not dry out.

Most vegetables reheat well provided they were not overcooked initially. Cover them to retain the moisture.

Bread can be reheated but watch the timing as it will be tough if overheated. A bread roll only needs about 10 seconds.

When preparing a meal on a plate arrange the thicker, denser foods round the outer edges, the delicate foods in the centre and try to keep to an even height. Cover with pierced cling film (plastic wrap) to keep the food moist.

Reheated pies will not become crisp as they do in the conventional cooker.

Timings will obviously vary with the quantity and temperature of the food. If you are uncertain how long to reheat a dish, microwave it for a minute or so. Check and repeat until the food is hot. Experience will soon tell you how long different foods take.

THAWING

One of the main attractions of the microwave is its ability to thaw frozen foods with ease and speed.

Apply the same techniques to thawing foods as you do to cooking them. In other words, turn, stir and shield them to equalise the heat and encourage even thawing. Standing time is just as important when thawing as it is when cooking. If large pieces of food are microwaved until the centre is thawed, the outer edges will start to cook.

Some foods, like vegetables, can be cooked from frozen and the following charts show where this is suitable.

Use the suggested timings as a guide only because the size and shape of the food and how deeply it has been frozen will affect the thawing times.

Remove any metal ties or foil wrappings and transfer any foods in foil containers to suitable dishes before thawing.

Melted ice should be drained off occasionally as it continues to attract microwave energy and will slow down the thawing.

◇ FISH ◇

Timings will depend on the size and thickness of fish and whether in a block or individual pieces. Separate blocks of fillets as soon as they are sufficiently thawed. Turn whole fish and shield tail ends if necessary. Thaw fish until it is still cold but pliable. Rinse off any ice crystals and stand for 5–10 minutes or until completely thawed. Cook as soon as possible after thawing.

FISH	TIME ON DEFROST (30%)	METHOD
Fish fillets		
225 g/8 oz	5–7 minutes	Place in a shallow dish. Cover. Separate and rearrange when partially thawed
450 g/1 lb	7–9 minutes	
Fish cutlets		
2 (100-g/4-oz)	4–5 minutes	Arrange thickest part to outer edge. Cover. Turn or rearrange once. Thickness varies so watch timing
4 (100-g/4-oz)	6–8 minutes	
Fish steaks		
2 (100-g/4-oz)	5–7 minutes	As above
4 (100-g/4-oz)	10–12 minutes	
Whole gutted fish:		
herring, trout, mackerel per 450 g/1 lb	4–8 minutes	Arrange head to tail. Cover. Rearrange and stand half-way through thawing. Shield tails if necessary
Prawns, shrimps, scampi, scallops		
225 g/8 oz	3–5 minutes	Turn into shallow dish. Stir once or twice. Drain. Use as soon as possible
450 g/1 lb	6–8 minutes	
Smoked salmon		
100 g/4 oz	1–1½ minutes	Unwrap and arrange slices on a plate. Cover

◇ POULTRY AND GAME ◇

Unwrap poultry and game and make sure any metal tags are removed. Thaw in a covered dish. Remove any giblets as soon as they are free. Thaw for half the recommended time, then stand for 10 minutes, covered, to allow the heat generated to spread. Shield any parts that feel warm. Stand until fully thawed and cook as soon as possible.

Very large birds are best thawed in the refrigerator as the surface may start to cook before the inside is thawed.

POULTRY AND GAME	TIME ON DEFROST (30%)	METHOD
Chicken		
pieces per 450 g/1 lb	7–9 minutes	Arrange with thickest part to edge of plate. Turn, shield if necessary. Stand for 10 minutes
whole per 450 g/1 lb	7–9 minutes	Turn several times. Remove giblets as soon as they are free. Stand for 10 minutes. Complete thawing time. Rinse. Stand for 20 minutes or until completely thawed
Duck per 450 g/1 lb	7–9 minutes	As for chicken
Game birds per 450 g/1 lb	5–8 minutes	As for chicken
Rabbit		
free-flow cubes per 450 g/1 lb	7–9 minutes	Turn into a dish, cover. Stir once or twice. Stand for 10 minutes
pieces per 450 g/1 lb	7–9 minutes	As for chicken pieces

POULTRY AND GAME	TIME ON DEFROST (30%)	METHOD
Turkey		
pieces per 450 g/1 lb	7–9 minutes	As for chicken pieces. Stand for 10 minutes
whole per 450 g/1 lb	8–10 minutes	Unwrap. Place breastside down. Cover. Turn several times. Shield where necessary. Remove from cooker, cover with foil and stand for 30 minutes twice during thawing. Rinse and give final standing time of 1 hour or until thawed
Venison (cubed) per 450 g/1 lb	7–9 minutes	Spread in a shallow dish. Cover. Stir during thawing. Stand for 5 minutes

MEAT AND OFFAL

If meat is not a uniform shape or size, shield the thinner ends with foil as soon as they are thawed so they don't start to cook. Large pieces should have a standing time half-way through the thawing to allow the generated heat to spread. If this is not done, the outside may start to cook before the inside has thawed. Wrap completely in foil for the standing time so heat is retained. Cook as soon as possible after thawing.

MEAT AND OFFAL	TIME ON DEFROST (30%)	METHOD
Joints or roasts per 450 g/1 lb	7–10 minutes	Place on dish. Cover. Turn. Stand large pieces for 20 minutes half-way through thawing. Stand for 30 minutes after thawing
Stewing cubes per 450 g/1 lb	7–9 minutes	Stand in shallow dish. Cover. Rearrange during thawing. Stand for 5 minutes
Minced or ground beef per 450 g/1 lb	8–9 minutes	Place in dish. Cover. Break up with a fork as it thaws, removing any softened areas as they will start to cook. Use immediately
Chops 4 (100-g/4-oz)	8–10 minutes	Place with thickest part to outside edge of plate. Cover. Rearrange during thawing. Stand for 5 minutes

MEAT AND OFFAL	TIME ON DEFROST (30%)	METHOD
Steaks 2 (225-g/8-oz)	5–7 minutes	Stand on plate. Cover. Turn over half-way through thawing. Stand fo 5 minutes
Liver per 450 g/1 lb	6–8 minutes	Place in a dish. Cover. If ir a block separate as soon a thawing allows. Turn. Stand for 5 minutes
Bacon		
rashers or slices 225 g/8 oz	2–3 minutes	Pierce the pack. Turn at half-time
joint (slab) vacuum-packed per 450 g/1 lb	8 minutes	Pierce the pack. Turn. Stand for 20 minutes
steaks 4 (100-g/4-oz)	7–9 minutes	Unwrap and separate when partially thawed. Stand for 5 minutes
Sausages		
thick per 450 g/1 lb	5–6 minutes	Unwrap and stand on a dish. Separate when partially thawed and arrange in a single layer. Turn. Stand for 5 minutes. Cook as soon as possible
thin per 450 g/1 lb	4–5 minutes	

◇ VEGETABLES ◇

Most vegetables can be cooked from frozen on full power. Small commercial packs can be cooked in their bags. Pierce the pouch and stand it in a dish. As it cannot be stirred, give it a shake during cooking. Stand vegetables for 2–3 minutes after microwaving to complete the cooking.

VEGETABLE	COOK ON FULL POWER	METHOD
Asparagus		
225 g/8 oz	7–9 minutes	Place in an oblong dish with 2 tablespoons water. Cover. Separate at half-time and arrange with heads to centre. Stand, drain and season
450 g/1 lb	10–12 minutes	
Beans		
broad (Lima)		
225 g/8 oz	5–7 minutes	Turn into a dish with 2 tablespoons water. Cover. Stir half-way through the cooking. Stand, drain and season
450 g/1 lb	7–9 minutes	
sliced green		
225 g/8 oz	5–6 minutes	Turn into a dish with 2 tablespoons water. Cover. Stir half-way through cooking. Stand, drain and season
450 g/1 lb	10–12 minutes	
whole green		
225 g/8 oz	5–6 minutes	Turn into a dish with 2 tablespoons water. Cover. Stir half-way through cooking. Stand, drain and season
450 g/1 lb	9–10 minutes	

VEGETABLE	COOK ON FULL POWER	METHOD
Broccoli		
225 g/8 oz free-flow	8–10 minutes	Arrange in a single layer if possible, with thick stalks to outer edge. Add 2 tablespoons water. Cover. Rearrange half-way through cooking. Stand, drain and season
450 g/1 lb free-flow	12–14 minutes	
Brussels sprouts		
button		
225 g/8 oz	6–7 minutes	Place in a dish with 2 tablespoons water. Cover. Stir once or twice. Stand, drain and season
450 g/1 lb	10–11 minutes	
medium		
225 g/8 oz	7–9 minutes	As above
450 g/1 lb	12–14 minutes	
Cabbage (chopped)		
225 g/8 oz	5–6 minutes	Turn into a dish or boiling bag with 2 tablespoons water. Stir or shake once. Stand, drain and season
450 g/1 lb	8–10 minutes	
Carots (sliced)		
225 g/8 oz	6–7 minutes	Place in a dish with 2 tablespoons water. Cover. Stir twice. Stand, drain and season
450 g/1 lb	12–13 minutes	
whole baby (small)		
225 g/8 oz	9–12 minutes	As above
450 g/1 lb	13–15 minutes	
Cauliflower florets		
225 g/8 oz	7–8 minutes	Cook in the same way as broccoli spears
450 g/1 lb	12–13 minutes	
Corn-on-the-cob		
two	6–7 minutes	Place in a dish with 2 tablespoons water. Cover. Turn at half-time, or with four rearrange them sides to middle. Stand, drain and season
four	9–11 minutes	

VEGETABLE	COOK ON FULL POWER	METHOD
Courgettes (Zucchini) (sliced) 225 g/8 oz 450 g/1 lb	 5–6 minutes 10–11 minutes	Spread out in a shallow dish. Cover. Stir once or twice. Stand, drain and pat dry on absorbent kitchen paper if adding to other dishes. Season
Leeks (sliced) 225 g/8 oz 450 g/1 lb	 5–6 minutes 8–10 minutes	Turn into a dish. Cover. Stir once or twice. Stand, drain and season
Mange-tout (snow) peas 225 g/8 oz 450 g/1 lb	 5–6 minutes 8–9 minutes	Turn into a dish with 2 tablespoons water. Cover. Stir twice. Stand, drain and season
Mushrooms (button) 225 g/8 oz	 5–6 minutes	Turn into a dish with 2 tablespoons water. Cover. Stir once. Stand, drain and season
Parsnipss (sliced) 225 g/8 oz 450 g/1 lb	 6–7 minutes 12–13 minutes	Turn into a shallow dish with 2 tablespoons water. Cover. Stir once or twice. Stand, drain and season
Peas 225 g/8 oz 450 g/1 lb	 4–5 minutes 8–9 minutes	Turn into dish with 2 tablespoons water. Cover. Stir once or twice. Stand, drain and season
Spinach (chopped) 225 g/8 oz 450 g/1 lb	 5–6 minutes 8–10 minutes	Turn into dish. Cover. Break down block and rearrange as it thaws. Stand, drain well and season
Sweetcorn kernels 225 g/8 oz 450 g/1 lb	 4–5 minutes 7–8 minutes	Turn into dish with 2 tablespoons water. Cover. Stir once or twice. Stand, drain and season

VEGETABLE	TIME ON DEFROST	METHOD
Onions (sliced)		
225 g/8 oz 450 g/1 lb	4–5 minutes 8 minutes	Turn into a shallow dish. Cover. Stir once or twice. Drain and pat dry on absorbent kitchen paper. They are now ready to fry or add to other dishes as required
Peppers (sweet bell) (sliced or diced)		
50 g/2 oz 100 g/4 oz	1–1½ minutes 2–2½ minutes	Can be added to stews frozen. Thaw as here for adding to rice or salads. Turn into dish. Cover. Stir once. Drain

FRUIT

Partially thaw fruits that need no cooking and then let them stand if serving cold. Soft fruits, in particular, will collapse if given too much microwave energy. If preferred cook from frozen, allowing about the same time as for defrosting but using full power.

FRUIT	TIME ON DEFROST (30%)	METHOD
Apples		
sliced		
225 g/8 oz 450 g/1 lb	3–4 minutes 7–8 minutes	Turn into a dish. Cover. Stir once or twice, gently separating if in a block. Stand for 5 minutes
purée		
300 ml/½ pint/1¼ cups 600 ml/1 pint/2½ cups	5—7 minutes 10–12 minutes	Unwrap and place in a dish. Cover. Break up and stir as block thaws, pushing frozen parts to outer edge
Blackberries		
25 g/8 oz 50 g/1 lb	4–5 minutes 6–7 minutes	Turn into dish. Cover. Stir once or twice. Stand for 5 minutes
Blackcurrants		
25 g/8 oz 50 g/1 lb	3–4 minutes 5–6 minutes	Turn into a dish. Cover. Stir once or twice. Stand for 5 minutes
Cherries		
25 g/8 oz 50 g/1 lb	4–5 minutes 6–8 minutes	Turn into a dish. Cover. Stir once or twice. Stand for 5 minutes
ruit juice		
75 ml/6 fl oz/¾ cup	1 minute ON FULL POWER	Turn into a jug. Break up with a spoon after 30 seconds

FRUIT	TIME ON DEFROST (30%)	METHOD
Fruit salad in syrup		
225 g/8 oz	6–7 minutes	Turn into dish. Cover. Separate fruits gently as block thaws. Complete thawing by standing rathe than oversoftening some c the fruits
450 g/1 lb	10–12 minutes	
Plums		
225 g/8 oz	5–6 minutes	Turn into a dish. Cover. Stir once or twice. If sizes vary some may thaw before others. Either remove them or stand the whole dish to complete thawing so smaller ones do not cook. Use as soon as possible as they discolour once thawed
450 g/1 lb	8–9 minutes	
Raspberries		
225 g/8 oz	3–4 minutes	Turn into a dish. Cover. Stir gently once or twice. Stand until no longer frosty
450 g/1 lb	5–6 minutes	
Rhubarb		
225 g/8 oz	5–6 minutes	Turn into a dish. Cover. Stir once or twice. Stand for 5 minutes
450 g/1 lb	8–9 minutes	
Strawberries		
225 g/8 oz	3–4 minutes	As raspberries
450 g/1 lb	5–6 minutes	

MISCELLANEOUS FOODS

Some of these foods only need thawing, others need heating. In each case the appropriate power level is given against the timing.

FOOD	TIMING	METHOD
Bread		
large loaf	7–8 minutes on defrost	Unwrap and stand in cooker. Turn once or twice. Stand for 10 minutes
small loaf	4–5 minutes on defrost	
one slice	20 seconds on defrost	Stand on absorbent kitchen paper
rolls		
two	1 minute on defrost	Stand them on absorbent kitchen paper
four	2 minutes on defrost	
pitta bread		
two pieces	2 minutes on defrost	Stand on absorbent kitchen paper.
four pieces	3 minutes on defrost	If thawing four, check half-way through as one may be ready and if not removed it will harden
Butter		
50 g/8 oz/1 cup	2 minutes on defrost	If foil-wrapped, remove and stand butter on dish. Turn once. Stand for 5 minutes
Cakes		
plain sponge	3 minutes on defrost	Unwrap cake and stand on absorbent kitchen paper. Turn once. Stand for 5 minutes
small cakes		
two	30–60 seconds on defrost	Place, uncovered, on plate. Check at half-time and remove any that are thawed. Stand for 2 minutes
four	1–1½ minutes on defrost	

FOOD	TIMING	METHOD
Éclairs		
two	45 seconds on defrost	Unwrap and stand on a plate. Don't thaw completely in microwave as chocolate will melt and cream run. Stand for 5–10 minutes
four	$1\frac{1}{2}$ minutes on defrost	
Cheese		
hard		This is not successful as after a very short period in the microwave the edges soften and change texture whilst the rest is still hard. Thaw at room temperature
soft		
75 g/3 oz block	$1\frac{1}{2}$–2 minutes on defrost	Remove foil wrapping. Place on a plate. Stand for 15 minutes
Cheesecake		
large (fruit-topped)	5–6 minutes on defrost	Remove from containers and stand on plate uncovered. If one area is softening too much remove the cheesecake and complete thawing at room temperature
small (fruit-topped)	1–$1\frac{1}{2}$ minutes on defrost	
Cream		
300 ml/$\frac{1}{2}$ pint/$1\frac{1}{4}$ cups	45 seconds on defrost. Stand for 5 minutes, 45 seconds on defrost	Remove carton lid or put pieces in a jug. It cannot be totally thawed in microwave as it starts to separate if overheated. Stand, stirring occasionally, until thawed
Flans or Quiches		
family size	Thaw/reheat 4–5 minutes on full power	Unwrap and remove foil container. Stand on absorbent kitchen paper or plate. Turn once. Stand for 3 minutes
individual size	Thaw/reheat $2\frac{1}{2}$–3 minutes on full power	
Mousse (individual)	Thaw 30 seconds on defrost	Remove lid. No standing time necessary

FOOD	TIMING	METHOD
Pancakes		
plain		
one	Thaw/reheat 45 seconds on full power	Place single pancake between greaseproof paper. Unwrap stack but leave interleaving paper. Rearrange as they soften, removing paper
eight	Thaw/reheat 4–5 minutes on full power	
stuffed		
two	Thaw/reheat 4–5 minutes on full power	Place in a dish. Cover. Turn or rearrange once. Stand for 2 minutes
four	Thaw/reheat 7–8 minutes on full power	
Pasta		
275 g/10 oz cooked weight (100 g/4 oz raw)	Thaw/reheat 4–5 minutes on full power	Turn into a dish. Cover. Stir once or twice. For large quantities heat it conventionally in a pan with boiling water just to cover. When water returns to the boil, pasta will be hot
Pastry (shortcrust [basic pie dough] and puff)		
1 small (212-g/7½-oz) packet	Thaw 1–1½ minutes on defrost	Leave pastry in wrapping. Turn once. Stand for 10 minutes.
1 medium (368-g/13-oz) packet	Thaw 1½–2 minutes on defrost	
Pizza		
family size	Thaw/reheat 3–4 minutes on full power	Unwrap and place on a plate. Turn once or twice. It will be soft not crisp as when conventionally heated
individual	Thaw/reheat 1½–2 minutes on full power	
Quiche		*See* Flans

TIPS

Apart from cooking you will also find your microwave invaluable for a number of food preparation and pre-cooking jobs.

◇ To soften butter or margarine for cake-making, put 100 g/4 oz/½ cup into a bowl large enough to hold the other ingredients and microwave on full power for 15–30 seconds.

◇ Melt chocolate by breaking 100 g/4 oz into pieces and putting into a bowl. Microwave on full power for 1–2 minutes. It retains its shape until touched.

◇ Cut a lemon in half, put it in a jug (pitcher) or bowl and microwave on full power for 1–2 minutes. The juice will pour out. Take care as the lemon will be very hot.

◇ Make dried breadcrumbs by standing a slice of bread on absorbent kitchen paper and microwaving on full power for 2–3 minutes. Check every minute as the timing will depend on the freshness of the bread. It will be brown through the middle if totally dry. Break up and crumb in a liquidiser or food processor or crush in a plastic bag with a rolling pin.

◇ To toast desiccated coconut, spread 100 g/4 oz/1 cup on a plate and microwave on full power for 5 minutes, stirring two or three times.

◇ Toast flaked almonds in the same way.

◇ When making preserves warm the bag of sugar on full power for 45 seconds. It will dissolve faster when added to the fruit.

◇ To make croûtons, cut 2 thick slices bread, trim off the crusts and spread both sides of each slice with softened butter. Cut into small cubes and spread over the base of a large plate or dish. Cook, uncovered, on full power for 3 minutes until firm to the touch, rearranging once. Spread out on absorbent kitchen paper to cool and crisp which will take about 1 minute.

◇ To soften gelatine, sprinkle 2–3 teaspoons powdered gelatine on to 3 tablespoons liquid and leave to sponge. Cook on full power for 30–45 seconds until dissolved. Stir and use.

◇ To make a brittle caramel for sprinkling over puddings, put 50 g/2 oz/2 tablespoons sugar in a dish with 2 tablespoons water and cook on full power for 1½ minutes. Stir well, until the sugar has dissolved. Continue cooking for a further 4–4½ minutes until golden. Watch the caramel carefully towards the end of the cooking time – if it gets too dark it will taste bitter. Have ready an oiled baking tray (sheet) or piece of foil and pour the caramel on to it in a thin layer. Leave until cold and lift it off the baking tray (sheet) or peel the foil away from the hardened caramel. Break up into pieces and use or store in an airtight container.

◇ Poppadums can be quickly crisped in the microwave though they will not colour as they do when grilled or fried (broiled or pan-fried). Place 2 poppadums on the floor of the microwave and cook on full power for about 1 minute until puffy. Stand on a wire rack to cool and crisp.

◇ To soften cabbage leaves for stuffing, remove one leaf at a time from a firm white or Savoy cabbage by cutting through the stalk (stem) at the base of the cabbage. Gently ease off the leaf. Continue round the cabbage taking off one outer leaf at a time. When you have removed 8 leaves put them in a bowl with 2 tablespoons water and cook on full power for 2–3 minutes until they are just pliable. Drain, cut out the thick piece of stalk (stem) at the base of each leaf and the leaves are ready for stuffing.

◇ Serve rusks with cheese as a change from bread or biscuits, making them from white or brown bread or bridge rolls. Slit 3 bridge rolls in half and arrange in a circle on the floor of the microwave. Cook on full power for 2 minutes until firm. Cool and crisp on a wire rack. Cut 1 cm/½ in thick slices of bread into rusk shapes. Place 6 in a circle on the floor of the microwave and cook on full power for 2–3 minutes. Timing will depend on the freshness of the bread but they are ready when firm and will crisp as they cool. Though the bread only colours through the middle, a mixture of brown, white and bridge rolls gives variety.

◇ Table jellies can be melted in the minimum of water then topped up with ice cold water for quicker setting. Put 3–4 tablespoons water in a bowl. Break the jelly tablet into it and heat on full power for 1½–2 minutes. Stir until completely dissolved, then top up to 600 ml/1 pint/2½ cups with cold water. Pour into a serving dish to set.

◇ Herbs can be successfully dried in the microwave. Wash, drain and dry about 25 g/1 oz leaves. Spread on a piece of absorbent kitchen paper and cover with another. Cook on full power for 2 minutes. Remove the top piece of kitchen paper and cook for a further 1–2 minutes. Timing will depend on the type of leaves and how dry they were at the start.

A–Z OF FOODS

• APPLES •

Apples particularly benefit from being cooked in a microwave. When sliced and stewed they emerge tender, translucent and with a marvellously heightened flavour of the fresh fruit. Choose firm, well-flavoured apples and they will cook beautifully in any of the traditional ways.

• BAKED •

The skins are tougher than when conventionally baked but the pulp is deliciously fruity.

2 APPLES Wipe and core 2 cooking (green) apples (about 225 g/8 oz each). Score the skins round the centre and stand them in a dish. Mix together 50 g/2 tablespoons demerara sugar and spoon it into the cavities. Sprinkle 3 tablespoons water, cider or apple juice in the dish. Leave uncovered and cook on full power for 4–6 minutes. Stand for 2 minutes.

4 APPLES Wipe and core 4 cooking (green) apples (about 225 g/8 oz each). Score the skins round the centre and stand them in a dish. Mix together 100 g/4 oz/1 cup chopped, tenderised, dried apricots with 50 g/2 oz/¼ cup demerara sugar and spoon it into the cavities. Sprinkle 4 tablespoons water, cider or apple juice in the dish. Leave uncovered and cook on full power for 9–11 minutes. Stand for 3 minutes.

Note If you find the apples have a tendency to burst, it may be because the concentrated sugar in the filling is attracting the microwaves and the consequent heat build-up results in uneven cooking. Next time try putting the filling mixture into the dish round the apples. Spoon it into the apples before serving.

• STEWED •

Peel, core and cut 450 g/1 lb eating apples into thick slices. Place the fruit in a dish with 50 g/2 oz/¼ cup sugar and the grated rind and juice of a small orange. Cover with cling film (plastic wrap), leaving a small gap for the steam to escape, and cook on full power for 2 minutes, stir and cook for a further 2–3 minutes. Stand for 3 minutes.

• PURÉED •

Peel, core and slice 450 g/1 lb cooking (green) apples. Place in a dish with 1 tablespoon lemon juice and 1 tablespoon water. Cover with cling film (plastic wrap), leaving a small gap for the steam to escape, and cook on full power for 3 minutes. Stir and cook for a further 3–4 minutes until soft and collapsed.

Sweet Apple Sauce

Beat the purée until smooth, stirring in 75–100 g/3–4 oz/$\frac{1}{3}$–$\frac{1}{2}$ cup sugar. Serve with milk puddings, cream or yogurt.

Savoury Apple Sauce

Beat the purée until smooth, stirring in 15 g/$\frac{1}{2}$ oz/1 tablespoon butter and 25 g/1 oz/2 tablespoons sugar and serve with duck, goose or pork.

Apple Snow

Cook and finish apples as for Sweet Apple Sauce and set aside to cool. Whisk 2 egg whites until firm, fold them into the cold apple sauce and divide between four wine glasses. Serve with crisp biscuits (cookies) or sponge fingers (Ladyfingers).

• APRICOTS •

Choose ripe fruits tending to be more orange than yellow as the flavour will be more developed. The fruit should be just softening but not mushy or bruised. Wash if necessary, wipe dry and remove any stalks. The apricots can be poached whole in syrup and served chilled with a few whole blanched almonds added just before serving. They can be halved, stoned (pitted) and cooked until tender, then filled into a pastry (pie) shell or puréed to use as a sauce, in sorbets, mousses or fools.

• POACHED WHOLE APRICOTS •

First, make the sugar syrup. Put 100 g/4 oz/$\frac{1}{2}$ cup sugar, 300 ml/$\frac{1}{2}$ pint/1$\frac{1}{4}$ cups water and 1 tablespoon lemon juice into a bowl. Cover with cling film (plastic wrap), leaving a small gap for the steam to escape, and cook on full power for 5–6 minutes, stirring once. Prick 450 g/1 lb prepared apricots to the kernel (pit) with a fork. Add them to the syrup, re-cover and cook on full power for 2 minutes. Stir and turn the fruits over in the syrup and cook for a further 2 minutes. Under-ripe fruit may need a little longer. Serve chilled.

• POACHED APRICOT HALVES •

Place 450 g/1 lb apricot halves in a dish with sugar syrup made as above but using only 50 g/2 oz/¼ cup sugar, 150 ml/¼ pint/⅔ cup water and 1 tablespoon lemon juice. Cover with cling film (plastic wrap), leaving a small gap for the steam to escape, and cook on full power for 2 minutes; stir and cook for a further 2–3 minutes. Keep on the firm side for use in a pie, a little softer for a purée. Stand for 3 minutes.

Apricot Tart or Pie

Arrange the cooled, drained apricot halves, cut side down in a pre-cooked pastry case (baked pie shell), over a bed of whipped cream or strained yogurt if liked. Microwave the juices on full power for 6–7 minutes until thick and syrupy. Spoon or brush this glaze over the fruit and leave to cool.

• APRICOT PURÉE •

Sieve the drained halves or purée in a liquidiser. Add as much of the syrup as is needed to sweeten and thin the purée.

• ARTICHOKES, GLOBE •

These cook quickly and well in the microwave. No pans of boiling water filling the kitchen with steam! Choose firm, plump artichokes with tightly closed leaves. Prepare them by cutting off the stalk close to the base of the leaves and breaking off any old and dry-looking leaves. Rinse in cold water and give the artichokes a shake.

To cook Place 4 artichokes upright in a bowl with 3 tablespoons salted water. Cover with cling film (plastic wrap), leaving a small gap for the steam to escape. Cook on full power for 12–14 minutes, rearranging half-way through the cooking. To check if they are ready, gently pull out one of the leaves; it should come away easily. Leave to stand for 3 minutes, then uncover and turn upside down to drain.

Serve hot with Hollandaise Sauce (see page 179) or melted butter, or cold with a vinaigrette made by blending together 3 tablespoons wine vinegar, 6 tablespoons olive oil and a seasoning of salt, freshly ground black pepper and ¼ teaspoon French (Dijon) mustard.

• ARTICHOKES, JERUSALEM •

Their gnarled and knobbly appearance belies the beauty of their delicate and delicious flavour which is fully retained when they are cooked in the microwave. Choose artichokes as evenly shaped as possible or there will be a lot of waste when preparing them. Peel (pare) and drop them into acidulated water (add 1 tablespoon lemon juice or vinegar to the bowl of water) as you go as they rapidly discolour when exposed to the air.

TO COOK Slice 450 g/1 lb prepared artichokes as near the same thickness as possible (a mixture of thick and thin slices will cook unevenly) into a dish. Sprinkle with 3 tablespoons water, cover with cling film (plastic wrap), leaving a small gap for the steam to escape, and cook on full power for 7–9 minutes, stirring half-way through the cooking. Let them stand for 3 minutes, then check. They should be firm but tender. Drain, season with a little salt, add a knob of butter if liked and serve.

If you prefer, they can be cut into 2.5-cm/1-in chunks and cooked on full power for 4–5 minutes.

ARTICHOKE AND PRAWN SALAD

Drain the cubed, cooked artichokes. Toss them in a French dressing while still warm. Chill and stir in 50–75 g/2–3 oz/1 cup peeled, cooked prawns (shrimps). Serve as a first course with crusty French bread.

• ASPARAGUS •

The easiest way to cook asparagus conventionally if you don't have a specially designed steamer is flat in a frying pan. However, this doesn't always produce the best results as the tips can be overcooked and watery before the stalks are ready. In the microwave asparagus only needs 4 tablespoons water to cook to an even tenderness and good flavour.

You want asparagus with tight well-formed heads and firm stalks. Bundles are usually size-graded but if you are buying it loose or picking your own, choose stalks of a similar thickness for even cooking.

Trim off the bottom woody section. Gently scrape the scales off the stalks, working from the head downwards. Only wash if necessary.

TO COOK Arrange 450 g/1 lb prepared asparagus in a flat oblong dish with the tips towards the centre as they cook more quickly than the stalks. Sprinkle with 4 tablespoons water, cover with cling film (plastic wrap), leaving a small gap for the steam to escape, and cook on full power for 8–10 minutes, rearranging the stalks half-way through the cooking time. Put the stalks from the sides to the middle and vice versa but keep the tips to the centre. Cooking time will vary with thickness and age. Thinner stalks will take a little less time, very thick ones may take a little longer. Drain and serve hot with melted butter or cold with a French dressing.

• AUBERGINES (EGGPLANTS) •

Choose firm aubergines with tight glossy skins avoiding any that are wrinkled or bruised. Cook them whole, whether they are to be sliced or puréed afterwards, and you will find they are a delicate pale green rather than a murky brown. If using them sliced, you may prefer to peel (pare) them as the skins can be tough and could spoil the finished dish.

It is often recommended that aubergines are salted before cooking. This is not always necessary though it does seem to reduce the amount of oil they absorb if they are to be fried or sautéd and with older vegetables it also releases some of the bitter juices. If you want to salt them, slice them into a colander, sprinkle with a little salt and leave to drain for about an hour. Rinse them well, pat dry and use.

TO COOK WHOLE Wipe or rinse and dry 2 aubergines (about 225 g/8 oz each) and trim the calyx off each. Prick several times with a fork. Place on a sheet of absorbent kitchen paper and cook on full power for 4–6 minutes until soft. Leave to cool before using.

TO COOK FOR SLICING Wipe or rinse and dry 2 aubergines (about 225 g/8 oz each), trim the calyx off each and peel them or not as you prefer. Place on a sheet of absorbent kitchen paper and cook on full power for 3–5 minutes, keeping them on the firm side. Stand for 1 minute, then slice through using a serrated knife. Serve as a vegetable or use in a moussaka.

AUBERGINE DIP

The usual way to cook aubergines whole for this dip is to grill (broil) them until the skin blackens. This gives them a smokey flavour lacking in the microwave version, which nevertheless is just as delicious. Cook 450 g/1 lb aubergines whole as above. When cool, halve and scoop out the flesh and purée it in a liquidiser or food processor together with 3 tablespoons olive oil, 2 tablespoons lemon juice, a crushed clove of garlic and a seasoning of salt and pepper. Spoon into a serving dish, cover with cling film (plastic wrap) and chill. Serve as a dip with raw vegetables or as a pâté with pitta or French bread.

• BACON •

• RASHERS (SLICES) •

These cook extremely well, from soft right through to crisp depending on your taste. Two or three rashers can be cooked on absorbent kitchen paper but this does have a tendency to stick to the bacon. Don't use it for a large quantity or you will find the rashers bonded to the paper before you can remove them. Instead use a rack so the fat can drain away and cover the bacon with absorbent kitchen paper to contain the spattering.

TIMING depends on the size and thickness of the rashers as

well as personal taste. The following is a rough guide to cooking on full power:

1 rasher	30–45 seconds	4 rashers	2–2½ minutes
2 rashers	1–1½ minutes	6 rashers	3½–4 minutes

If you need bacon that's snappily crisp for salads or toppings, cook for a further 30 seconds or so depending on size and number of rashers.

• JOINTS (SLABS) •

Check with your supplier – or the instructions on the label – if the piece needs soaking in cold water before cooking. Sweet-cure (Canadian) bacon is mild and should not need it, but some cures and certain cuts can be quite salty and benefit from a few hours' soaking. If the bacon is particularly salty, you will find the outer edges harden during cooking.

TIMING about 7–8 minutes per 450 g/1 lb.

TO COOK Place a 1-kg/2-lb piece in a roasting bag and tie loosely with string or an elastic band. Place in a dish and cook on full power for 8 minutes. Turn over and cook for a further 8 minutes. Stand tented with foil for 10 minutes. A microwave thermometer will ensure it is cooked to the right temperature if you have any doubts.

• BEANS •

Choose only young firm beans which will retain their fresh bright colour and taste – tender with a hint of crispness. If you prefer a totally soft bean, you will be happier with them conventionally cooked.

• BROAD (LIMA) •

Young tender beans cook well but avoid older, larger ones as the skins can be very tough. Put 450 g/1 lb shelled beans into a dish with 4 tablespoons water. Cover with cling film (plastic wrap), leaving a small gap for the steam to escape, and cook on full power for 8–10 minutes, stirring after 3 minutes. Check frequently as cooking time depends on age and size of bean. Overcooking will harden the beans and toughen the skins.

• DRIED •

These need time to rehydrate so soaking is always necessary and little time is saved by cooking them in the microwave.

See PULSES.

• DWARF AND FRENCH (GREEN) •

Wash, top and tail 450 g/1 lb beans. Place in a dish with 4 tablespoons water, cover with cling film (plastic wrap), leaving a small gap for the steam to escape, and cook on full power for 5–9 minutes. Stir after 3 minutes. Drain and season with salt and pepper.

• RUNNER •

Wash 450 g/1 lb beans, string if necessary and cut into thick slices. Put into a dish with 4 tablespoons water. Cover with cling film (plastic wrap), leaving a small gap for the steam to escape, and cook on full power for 10–12 minutes, stirring once or twice. Stand for 3 minutes, drain, season and serve. Timing will depend on age and freshness of the beans and how thickly they are cut, but expect them to be crisp rather than soft.

• BEEF •

Beef cooked in the microwave, though moist and succulent, will not have the rich brown colour and crispy surface of a conventionally roasted joint (piece). Cooking in the microwave followed by a short time in a hot oven produces the best results. As your oven will probably be on for the traditional accompaniments of Yorkshire pudding and roast potatoes, this works extremely well – cutting down on roasting time but still producing a succulent well-browned piece of meat.

Choose only the tender roasting joints such as sirloin and rolled rib and make sure that they are as evenly shaped as possible. Irregular shapes cook unevenly and parts may need shielding with small pieces of foil to prevent overcooking.

You will need to lift the meat off the base of the dish so that it does not cook in its own juices. Do this in one of the following ways:

☐ stand it on a roasting rack over a shallow dish and cover it with a slit roasting bag tented over it.

☐ stand the meat on one, or if necessary two, upturned plain saucers or a plate and cover with a slit roasting bag tented over it.

☐ stand the meat on a rack inside a roasting bag and tie the bag loosely with a piece of string or an elastic band. Place in a dish.

The meat should be turned over at half-time and the fats and juices drained off because they attract microwave energy away from the meat.

TIMING about 5–6 minutes per 450 g/1 lb for rare beef; 6–7 minutes per 450 g/1 lb for medium beef; 7–8 minutes per 450 g/1 lb for well-done beef. For greater accuracy use a microwave thermometer. This is sold with a chart giving two temperatures for all meats: the first is the temperature it should have reached at the end of the cooking time and the second the temperature it should reach after standing.

TO COOK A JOINT/PIECE OF MEAT Place a 1.5-kg/3-lb piece of sirloin on a roasting rack and cover with a lid or slit a roasting bag down one side and place loosely over the meat. Cook on full power for 15 minutes, turning over half-way through the cooking. Remove the bag and transfer the meat to a roasting tin (pan) with a little of the juices. Season with salt and pepper and roast in a hot oven (220 C, 425 F, gas 7) for about 15 minutes. This will give you meat that is brown on the outside and rare in the centre. Cook for 30 minutes in the oven if you prefer the beef cooked through.

Use the collected juices to make gravy while the roast finishes cooking. Spoon 2–3 tablespoons of the meat fat and juices into a jug (pitcher) or bowl. Stir in 15 g/½ oz/2 tablespoons flour to make a smooth paste or use 1 tablespoon gravy powder blended to a paste with cold water. Gradually blend in 300 ml/½ pint/1¼ cups hot beef stock. Cook on full power, stirring once or twice, for 3–4 minutes, until thickened.

• BRAISING AND POT ROASTING •

Here a piece of beef is cooked with a small amount of liquid and a selection of flavouring vegetables. Unless a prime cut is used, it should be tenderised by marinating for several hours or be pricked deeply all over with a fork or skewer. Little time is saved and you may find the flavour is not as good as when conventionally cooked.

TO COOK Place the prepared 1 kg/2 lb meat in a roasting bag with 150 ml/¼ pint/⅔ cup liquid (stock, tomato juice or wine) and a quartered onion, a carrot cut into chunks, a sliced leek and a celery stick (stalk). Partially close the bag with a piece of string or an elastic band. Place in a dish and cook on low power or 'defrost' for 1½ hours, turning over half-way through. Depending on the quality of the meat, it may take even longer to cook. Serve with freshly cooked vegetables and the meat juices. These can be thickened by sieving with the flavouring vegetables.

• STEWING •

By using low power (30%) it is possible to cook stews in the microwave, though if the meat is tough it will be no quicker than cooking conventionally. Careful preparation of the meat is important: cut it either into small strips or cubes and prick it all over or marinate it to help tenderise it. The time taken will be anything between 1–2 hours depending on the quality of the meat.

The meat does not seem to absorb the flavours of the vegetables and liquids in the way it does when conventionally cooked. Certainly if left to stand overnight and then reheated, the flavour is considerably improved but it is scarcely quick cooking.

A traditional stew, which uses the tougher but tastier cuts of beef together with a selection of root vegetables and seasonings, and is conventionally cooked very slowly over a gentle heat, allows the flavours to develop, mingle and enrich the whole and produces far superior results.

• MINCED/GROUND BEEF •

This cooks extremely well in the microwave and browns quite acceptably without pre-frying.

TO COOK Put 1 tablespoon oil and a finely chopped, small onion into a bowl and cook on full power for 3–4 minutes until the onion has softened. Stir in 450 g/1 lb mince/ground beef breaking it up well. Cover with cling film (plastic wrap), leaving a small gap for the steam to escape, and cook on full power for 5 minutes, stirring once. Drain off the surplus fat, then stir in a tablespoon each of flour and (mild) paprika, 150 ml/$\frac{1}{4}$ pint/$\frac{2}{3}$ cup tomato juice and a seasoning of salt and pepper. Cover again with cling film (plastic wrap), leaving a small gap for the steam to escape, and cook on full power for 5 minutes.

This is a well-flavoured mixture that can either be served on its own topped with mashed potatoes for a shepherd's pie or with dumplings. It is infinitely adaptable. Use beef stock in place of tomato juice and season with a dash of Worcestershire sauce. Turn it into a chilli con carne by adding a small chopped (bell) pepper with the onion, using chilli powder in place of the paprika and stirring in 1 (397-g/14-oz) can or 2 cups canned tomatoes and the same amount of drained kidney beans.

• STEAKS •

These need a browning dish to give them eye appeal. If you have several to do, entailing reheating the browning dish, it would be quicker to use the grill or frying pan (broiler or skillet).

• FLASH FRY STEAKS •

These are cheaper than traditional steaks and can be used successfully in the microwave for such dishes as beef stroganoff.

• BEEFBURGERS •

These can be cooked on a plate or shallow dish. If they appear rather fatty, it is worth using a rack so the fat can drain away. Good flavour and texture; they brown quite well. For a crisper, darker burger, use a browning dish or cook conventionally.

The ones tested were fresh, all beef and weighed 100 g/4 oz/$\frac{1}{4}$ lb each.

2 beefburgers: stand on rack, cover with absorbent kitchen paper and cook on full power for 4–6 minutes.

4 beefburgers: stand on rack, cover with absorbent kitchen paper and cook on full power for 6–9 minutes.

Stand for 2 minutes before serving.

• BEETROOT (BEETS) •

These cook perfectly in only a few spoonfuls of water with no loss of colour or flavour. No more steamy kitchens or stained pans! Wash the beetroots and trim off the stalks.

TO COOK Prick 2 beetroots (about 225 g/8 oz each) with a fork and place in a dish with 3 tablespoons water. Cover with cling film (plastic wrap), leaving a gap for the steam to escape, and cook on full power for 5 minutes. Turn and cook for a further 7–8 minutes. Stand for 5 minutes, uncover and peel (pare). Skins should just rub off when fully cooked.

• BISCUITS (COOKIES) •

Biscuits are not totally successful in the microwave. You cannot achieve an evenly shaped, crisply golden biscuit. Soft mixtures spread and spread resulting in very thin biscuits with a rather more chewy texture. Interesting, but they taste and look nothing like the same mixture baked conventionally.

However, a refrigerator cookie that is shaped into a roll and sliced works quite well. The shape will not be perfect but by using brown sugar you get a good flavour and colour. Worth trying. Keep the roll in the refrigerator, wrapped in cling film (plastic wrap) or foil, and you can slice and bake them as they are needed. The mixture can be left plain or be flavoured as suggested in the recipe below which makes about 36 biscuits.

Refrigerator Cookies

Cream 150 g/5 oz/1 cup soft brown sugar with 150 g/5 oz/¾ cup softened butter or margarine. Stir in a beaten egg yolk, then gradually work in 225 g/8 oz/2¼ cups flour.

Divide the dough into three. Work a few chopped nuts into one piece and shape it into a roll about 5 cm/2 in wide and 7.5 cm/3 in long. Work 2 teaspoons (unsweetened) cocoa powder into a thick paste with a little water and blend this into the second piece. Don't worry if it is a bit streaky – it looks quite attractive when cooked. Shape into a roll as before. It will be softer and stickier but will firm up in the refrigerator. Leave the last piece of dough plain and shape into a roll as above. Wrap each roll in foil and refrigerate until quite firm.

Cut six (5-mm/¼-in) slices off the dough and arrange in a circle on a plate. Cook straight from the refrigerator on full power for 3 minutes. Leave to stand for 1 minute, then transfer to a wire (cake) rack. When cold they will have a pleasant crunchy chewiness.

• BLACKBERRIES •

Buy or pick whole, firm, deeply-coloured blackberries. Hull and wash them if necessary in a colander under running cold water. Drain.

To cook Turn 450 g/1 lb blackberries into a dish. Sprinkle the fruit with 75 g/3 oz/⅓ cup sugar, cover with cling film (plastic wrap), leaving a small gap for the steam to escape, and cook on full power for 4–6 minutes, stirring half-way through the cooking. Stand for 3 minutes.

• BLACKCURRANTS •

Choose firm, fully ripe fruit, remove any stalks and rinse in a colander under running cold water. Drain.

To cook Put 450 g/1 lb blackcurrants in a dish with 2 tablespoons water and 100 g/4 oz/½ cup sugar. Cover with cling film (plastic wrap), leaving a small gap for the steam to escape, and cook on full power for 5–6 minutes, stirring once. Check to see if they need further sweetening and if so, stir in a little more sugar which will dissolve in the heat of the juices. Stand for 3 minutes.

Blackcurrant Whip

Mash 2 ripe bananas in a bowl and stir in 3–4 tablespoons blackcurrants cooked as above and cooled. Stir in 300 ml/½ pint/1 cup natural (plain) yogurt. Lightly whip 150 ml/¼ pint/½ cup double (heavy) cream and fold through the fruit and yogurt. Serve chilled.

• BLUEBERRIES •

These are plump, dark blue berries available fresh in the late summer or frozen all the year. When preparing fresh ones, remove any stalks and leaves, rinse in a colander under running cold water and drain. They can be used in pies and crumbles without any preliminary cooking or stewed in the same way as blackcurrants (above).

• BREAD •

Microwaved bread, it must be said, compares unfavourably with a conventionally baked loaf in texture, taste and appearance. The texture is rather closer and overcooking will produce a tough crumb. Although sprinkling with seeds, grains and nuts will add some flavour, this is primarily a cosmetic job to disguise the lack of golden crust.

Emergencies, however, arise and if you have no standby loaf in the freezer, a packet of bread mix will enable you to produce a loaf in about 45 minutes. Wholewheat flour is a better choice than white. It looks more appetising and has much more flavour. Jugs (pitchers), bowls or round dishes make good containers. Bread cooked in loaf dishes has a tendency to harden at the corners if even slightly overcooked.

The following recipe uses more liquid than recommended on the packet but when microwaving this produces a lighter, moister more open-textured loaf. It's best eaten fresh and still warm though it responds well to toasting the next day.

Wholewheat or Granary Loaf

Tip a (280-g/10-oz) packet Brown Bread Mix into a food processor or bowl. Add 300 ml/½ pint/1¼ cups hand-hot water and mix well until smooth and elastic. This will only take 1 minute in a food processor. Turn the soft mixture into a bowl or jug (pitcher). If you have a 2-litre/3½-pint/4½-pint jug (pitcher), like the ones recommended for making sauces in the microwave, this works perfectly giving a nice shape to the loaf. Otherwise use a pudding basin (bowl) which gives a similar shape.

Cover and leave in a warm place until doubled in size which will take about 30 minutes. Uncover and cook on full power for 5 minutes. Stand for 2 minutes and turn out. The surface will be a little damp but will dry off as it stands. Put under the grill (broiler) for a couple of minutes if you feel it needs it.

If you have even less time to spare, then a rather good soda bread can be made in little more than 15 minutes.

Soda Bread

Sift together into a bowl 225 g/8 oz/2 cups white or wholemeal flour, ½ teaspoon bicarbonate of soda, 1 teaspoon cream of tartar and ½ teaspoon salt. Rub in 25 g/1 oz/2 tablespoons butter and gradually work in 150 ml/¼ pint/⅔ cup half milk and half water to form a soft dough. You may need a little less or a spoonful more; it depends on the flour.

Pat into a flattish round about 13 cm/5 in across and score with a deep cross. Stand on a greased dish and cook on full power for 4 minutes. Stand for 2 minutes and turn out on to a rack cross side up. Grill (broil) for a few moments to brown the top.

If made with white flour, the soda bread really does need a couple of minutes under the grill to brown its craggy top. It then looks as good as it tastes. It has a slightly cakey texture which is as it should be.

• BROCCOLI •

Choose only broccoli spears that are young and fresh with firm green or purple florets. Once they have begun to yellow and age, both texture and flavour are spoilt and, when cooked in the microwave, they taste unpleasantly strong. Prepare the broccoli by removing leaves and cutting off the very thick part of the stalk. Divide into florets of roughly the same size and wash them.

To cook Arrange 225 g/8 oz broccoli in a dish with the heads to the centre. Add 3 tablespoons water, cover with cling film (plastic wrap), leaving a small gap for the steam to escape, and cook on full power for 5–6 minutes, rearranging the broccoli half-way through the cooking. Stand for 2 minutes. Drain and season.

• BRUSSELS SPROUTS •

Choose fresh, tightly-closed green sprouts avoiding any that are yellowing or wilted and all roughly the same size. If you have a mixture of large and tiny ones, they will cook unevenly. Trim off any damaged leaves and wash.

TO COOK Put 450 g/1 lb into a dish with 6 tablespoons water. Cover with cling film (plastic wrap), leaving a small gap for the steam to escape, and cook on full power for 7–10 minutes. They should be firm but tender. If you want to purée them, cook for a minute or two longer until softer, adding a little more water if necessary. Drain and whizz them up in a liquidiser or food processor with a spoonful or two of cream, a tablespoon of butter and a seasoning of salt and pepper.

• CABBAGE •

It's no quicker to cook cabbage crisply in the microwave but the flavour is good and there's no pan to wash. Both the white Dutch cabbage and the crinkly green Savoy take about the same time to cook, though the latter can be tough.

TO COOK Put 450 g/1 lb prepared cabbage in a large dish with 3 tablespoons water. Cover with cling film (plastic wrap), leaving a small gap for the steam to escape, and cook on full power for 8–10 minutes. Stir once or twice during cooking. Drain, season and serve.

• RED CABBAGE •

This is usually cooked with apples and seasoning for anything up to 2 hours in the oven. In the microwave it will take 20 minutes and taste just as good. It reheats beautifully with, if anything, an improved and mellowed flavour. Prepare by removing any damaged or wilted leaves. Halve and quarter the cabbage, remove the hard centre and shred as much as needed. Store the rest in cling film (plastic wrap) in the refrigerator.

To cook Put a small chopped onion and 1 tablespoon oil in a large dish and cook on full power for 2 minutes. Stir in 450 g/1 lb shredded red cabbage, together with 1 peeled, cored and chopped cooking (green) apple, 2 tablespoons demerara sugar and 3 tablespoons red wine vinegar. Cover with cling film (plastic wrap), leaving a small gap for the steam to escape, and cook on full power for 10 minutes. Stir and cook for a further 10 minutes. Season with salt and pepper, giving it all a good stir. It can be eaten immediately or left to stand and reheated.

• CAKES •

You can cook cakes in the microwave but they will not turn out like your conventional baked ones. This is because microwaving is a moist form of cooking and baking by definition is 'cooking by dry heat'. So a plain sponge will be well risen and moist but will lack the golden colour and firm crisp surface of a conventionally baked one.

The cakes that work best are the naturally moist ones – gooey chocolate cakes and sticky gingerbread – with the ingredients providing a good rich colour. This type of recipe also looks appetising. Bearing in mind the limitations, experiment with some of your favourite recipes to discover those that you find acceptable.

The following guidelines will ensure that you get the best possible results:

◇ Remember that a moist mixture is the most successful so add a spoonful or two of milk or water to give a softer than usual consistency. It should drop quite easily from the spoon without having to be shaken off.

◇ Cakes rise spectacularly in the microwave so make sure the container is large enough to take the extra rising or the mixture will spill over. The dish should be no more than half full.

◇ You cannot of course use metal cake tins (pans) in the microwave but ovenproof glass is excellent. It should be lightly greased and the base lined with greaseproof (waxed) paper.

◇ The specially designed re-usable plastic containers need no greasing and are sufficiently flexible to press or bend to help the cake out if necessary.

◇ Small cakes can be cooked in double thickness paper cases standing in a muffin dish or ramekin dishes (custard cups).

◇ A ring mould is the ideal shape for a cake because it allows the mixture to cook more evenly. Round dishes also work well provided you remember that the centre is the last part to cook.

◇ Test if a cake is done by piercing it with a wooden cocktail stick (toothpick) half-way between the edge and centre. If it comes out clean the cake is ready even if the centre appears moist.

◇ The most difficult thing to get used to is removing cakes from the microwave with the surface still moist. But do so and you will find that after something like 5 minutes' standing time it will have dried out. If it hasn't, it can always be given extra cooking time. Undercooking can be remedied. Overcooking results in a dry and seemingly stale cake.

• CANDIES •

See SWEETS.

• CARROTS •

Choose firm fresh carrots, avoiding any that are soft. Scrape or peel them (pare thinly) and slice into rings. Whole baby new (small young) carrots can be trimmed, washed and left whole.

TO COOK SLICED CARROTS Put 450 g/1 lb sliced carrots into a dish with 3 tablespoons water. Cover with cling film (plastic wrap), leaving a small gap for the steam to escape, and cook on full power for 10–12 minutes, stirring once or twice. Stand for 3 minutes. Drain and season.

WHOLE BABY (SMALL YOUNG) CARROTS Put 225 g/8 oz prepared carrots in a dish with 25 g/1 oz/2 tablespoons butter. Cover with cling film (plastic wrap), leaving a small gap for the steam to escape, and cook on full power for 5–7 minutes. Stand for 2 minutes. Season and serve.

• CAULIFLOWER •

Choose a cauliflower that has a firm, tightly closed head of white florets surrounded by fresh-looking green leaves. Avoid any that are limp or discoloured as they are likely to taste unpleasantly strong. Remove the leaves and trim the stalk. Wash well and shake off surplus water.

TO COOK A WHOLE CAULIFLOWER Stand a medium cauliflower in a dish stem upwards and cover with cling film (plastic wrap), leaving a small gap for the steam to escape. Cook on full power for 6–8 minutes, turning over half-way through the cooking time. Stand for 3 minutes. The cooked cauliflower should be firm but tender.

TO COOK FLORETS Place 450 g/1 lb florets in a dish, cutting any large ones in half so they are all roughly the same size. Add 3 tablespoons water and cover with cling film (plastic wrap), leaving a small gap for the steam to escape. Cook on full power for 9–11 minutes, stirring half-way through the cooking. Stand for 2 minutes, drain, season and serve.

• CELERIAC •

This is a root variety of celery with a brown fibrous skin and crisp white flesh, which should be firm and undamaged with no traces of sponginess. It can be used in salads or it makes a delicious cooked vegetable with its delicate but distinct flavour of celery. It can be cooked, seasoned and tossed in butter before serving. It can be cooked and mashed to serve as a purée or cooked, mashed and mixed with half its weight in mashed potatoes as a topping to a shepherd's pie. Perhaps the nicest way of all is to cut it into small chunks (dice), cook, then toss in butter and sprinkle with grated cheese and grill (broil) until brown and bubbling. For a salad try the Celeriac Rémoulade below.

To prepare celeriac, wash and halve it, then remove the skin. It is easier to do this when it is cut so you can see just how thickly it needs peeling (paring). Slice or cube into acidulated water (1 tablespoon vinegar to 1.15 litres/2 pints/2½ pints water) to prevent it discolouring

TO COOK Drain 450 g/1 lb prepared celeriac and put in a dish with 3 tablespoons water. Cover with cling film (plastic wrap), leaving a small gap for the steam to escape, and cook on full power for 7–10 minutes, stirring half-way through. Stand for 2 minutes. Drain and season and use in any of the ways suggested above. If cooking 225 g/8 oz it will take 4–6 minutes.

Celeriac Rémoulade

Cut 225 g/8 oz prepared celeriac into matchstick strips. Put into a dish with 2 tablespoons water. Cover with cling film (plastic wrap), leaving a small gap for the steam to escape, and cook on full power for 2 minutes to blanch. Tip into a colander and cool under running cold water. Drain and dry on absorbent kitchen paper. Mix 4 tablespoons mayonnaise with 2 teaspoons Dijon mustard and stir the celeriac into it. This dish tastes good with cold cooked ham.

• CELERY •

Though more usually served raw with cheese or in salads, celery makes a good cooked vegetable providing it is carefully prepared. That means removing all the stringy bits. Choose celery that is firm and unblemished with pale green straight leaves. Trim the root and break off the green leaves, pulling any strings away with them. Any particularly tough outer sticks (stalks) and the leaves can be used for flavouring stocks or casseroles. Cut the remaining sticks (stalks) into 7.5-cm/3-in lengths, pulling off any more strings as you cut it.

To cook Put 4 tablespoons salted water into a dish and add 450 g/1 lb prepared celery sticks (stalks). Cover with cling film (plastic wrap), leaving a small gap for the steam to escape, and cook on full power for 7–10 minutes, stirring half-way through the cooking. Stand for 3 minutes, drain and serve.

• CHEESE •

Cheese is a protein food, rich in fat, and needs gentle cooking if it isn't to toughen and become stringy. Full power can be used for melting cheese providing you keep checking it to see that parts aren't overcooking. Slowing down the process by using a medium or lower power often produces a better result. If your cooker has variable power, follow the manufacturers' instructions for cheese cookery.

Cream and soft cheeses firm from the refrigerator can be microwaved on 'defrost' for 15–30 seconds to soften them. Don't forget to remove any foil wrappings.

Welsh Rarebit

Blend ½ teaspoon mustard powder with 3 tablespoons beer in a medium bowl. Season with a little salt and pepper, then stir in 175 g/6 oz/2 cups grated mature Cheddar cheese. Leave uncovered and cook on low power (30%) for 1½ minutes. Stir and cook for a further 1 minute. Stir and blend. Spread on 4 slices of toast and grill (broil) until brown. If all the mixture is not needed, cover it and store in the refrigerator for a few days.

• CHERRIES •

Most cherries only need a brief cooking to tenderise them – particularly the large, fleshy black ones. The amount of sweetening will depend on the variety.

Choose firm undamaged cherries, remove any stalks and wash. Stone (pit) them if you like.

To cook Place 450 g/1 lb cherries in a dish with 50–100 g/2–4 oz/¼–½ cup sugar, cover with cling film (plastic wrap), leaving a small gap for steam to escape. Cook on full power for 3–5 minutes. Stand for 3 minutes. Serve hot or cold.

A compote of cherries makes a lovely summer dessert. Cook them like apricots (see page 183) in a sugar syrup using red wine in place of water. Serve cold with vanilla ice cream.

• CHICK PEAS •

Chick peas are much the same size and shape as hazelnuts and are widely available dried and canned. The dried ones usually need soaking overnight before cooking but microwaving can shorten this time (see PULSES).

Canned chick peas are an even speedier alternative. Turn 1 (410-g/14½-oz) can chick peas into a dish, cover with cling film (plastic wrap), leaving a small gap for the steam to escape, and cook on full power for 2–3 minutes, drain and use.

These can be stirred into a cooked stew. Alternatively, they can be mixed with an equal quantity of freshly cooked pasta shapes and served with butter or oil and Parmesan cheese to make the Italian dish known as Thunder and Lightning.

Chick peas can be tossed in a French dressing and sprinkled with chopped parsley and spring onions to serve as a cold salad.

The beans absorb the flavour of the dressing better if tossed in it whilst warm.

• CHICKEN •

Chicken cooked in the microwave has beautifully moist flesh but the skin remains soft and pallid. For a bird that is to be cut up cold for salads or sandwiches or used in a made-up dish later, this does not matter as the skin can be discarded. But for a chicken that is to be carved and served hot it looks singularly unappetising. Brushing with colourants or sauces improves its appearance but can also add unnecessary flavours. Get the best of both worlds by microwaving to ensure tender moist flesh, then transferring the bird to a hot oven for a crisp brown skin.

TIMING about 6–8 minutes per 450 g/1 lb.

• PERFECT ROAST CHICKEN •

Remove the giblets from a 1.5-kg/3½-lb chicken. Remove any pieces of fat from just inside the cavity and rinse well. Dry the chicken with absorbent kitchen paper. Truss the chicken to hold wings and legs close to the body using wooden (never metal) skewers or string.

It needs to be raised out of its juices during cooking so stand it on a roasting rack or an upturned saucer in a dish breast side down. Covering is not absolutely necessary though it does contain any spattering. Use a roasting bag or greaseproof (waxed) paper. Cook for 10 minutes on full power. Drain off the juices. Turn the chicken breast side up. Shield the wing and leg tips if necessary with small pieces of foil. Make sure the foil cannot touch the cooker walls. Cook for a further 10 minutes on full power. Transfer the chicken to a roasting tin (pan). Baste with a little of the fats, season with salt and pepper and roast in a hot oven (220 C, 425 F, gas 7) for about 15 minutes until crisp and golden.

To test if the chicken is cooked, insert the tip of a sharp knife between the thigh and body. The juices should run clear and the flesh be opaque. If the juices are pink, cook a little longer. Another test is to pull the leg gently from the body; if it shows no signs of resistance, it is cooked. If using a thermometer, remember to put it into the thickest part of the thigh but not touching the bone.

• BOILING CHICKENS •

Don't cook these in the microwave. They are much older and tougher birds and need long, slow conventional cooking to tenderise them.

• CHICKEN PIECES •

These cook well in the microwave and take about 8 minutes per 450 g/1 lb. If they are to be eaten plain, give them a few minutes under the grill (broiler) to crisp and brown the skin. Try to choose pieces of a similar size for even cooking or be prepared to remove any smaller pieces as they are cooked. A portioned chicken will obviously produce pieces of varying shapes and thicknesses and you will need to rearrange them during cooking.

When cooking chicken pieces in a sauce, remove the skin and any fat first or the sauce will be greasy. This also enables the flavourings to penetrate the flesh better. Make sure the sauce covers the pieces and move them around during cooking.

Chicken Marengo

Put 2 tablespoons oil and 1 finely chopped, medium onion into a dish large enough to take a 1.5-kg/3½-lb chicken cut into pieces. Cook on full power for 3 minutes. Stir 2 tablespoons flour into the onion, then gradually stir in 4 tablespoons white wine, the contents of 1 (397-g/14-oz) can/2 cups canned tomatoes, 100 g/4 oz/1 cup sliced mushrooms and a seasoning of salt and pepper. Stir well and add the skinned chicken pieces, making sure they are covered by the sauce and arranging them with the thickest parts to the outside of the dish. Cover with cling film (plastic wrap), leaving a small gap for the steam to escape, and cook on full power for 25 minutes. Stir and re-position the chicken twice during cooking. Check seasoning and serve.

• CHICKEN LIVERS •

Take care not to overcook or they will toughen. They should still be slightly pink inside. Trim, halve and wash the livers. Pat dry on absorbent kitchen paper. Put 25 g/1 oz/2 tablespoons butter in a dish and heat on full power for 30–45 seconds until melted. Add the chicken livers and turn them in the butter. Cover with cling film (plastic wrap), leaving a small gap for the steam to escape, and cook for 2 minutes. Stir and cook for another minute if not quite ready. Stand for 2 minutes. Spoon on to hot buttered toast, stir into a dish of cooked pasta or add to a tossed green salad just prior to serving.

• CHICORY •

The conical white heads tipped with yellow should be firm, the leaves tightly packed, none of them wilting or browning. If the chicory has turned green, it means it has been exposed to the light, will taste bitter and should be avoided. Remove a thin slice from the root end and, with a pointed knife, cut out the core. Rinse the heads under running cold water.

TO COOK Place 4 medium heads chicory in a dish head to tail. Add 1 tablespoon each of water and lemon juice. Cover with cling film (plastic wrap), leaving a small gap for the steam to escape, and cook on full power for 5–7 minutes. Drain, season, toss in a little melted butter and serve.

• CHINESE LEAVES •

Chinese leaves look rather like a pale cos lettuce, though heavier and more tightly packed. The leaves can be shredded and used raw in salads or cooked briefly so they retain their fresh crispness.

Slice by holding the head tightly together and, starting from the open end, cut across into shreds. Slice as much as you need, then store the rest in a plastic bag in the refrigerator. It will keep for a week.

TO COOK Put 450 g/1 lb prepared leaves in a large ovenproof bowl with 3 tablespoons water, cover with cling film (plastic wrap), leaving a small gap for the steam to escape, and cook on full power for 5–7 minutes, stirring once. Drain, season and serve.

• CHIPS (FRENCH FRIES) •

See POTATOES.

• CHOUX PASTRY (PASTE) •

This is the pastry used for making éclairs and choux buns. It cannot be cooked in the microwave. It needs dry heat to puff and crisp it.

• CHUTNEY AND RELISHES •

The microwave is ideal for making small quantities of chutney and relishes. The ingredients don't stick and are unlikely to burn because there is no direct heat to the bowl. You need an ovenproof bowl that is large enough for the ingredients to bubble hard without boiling over. The fruits and vegetables should be finely chopped or minced (ground), then cooked with the sugar, vinegar and flavouring ingredients to a thick sauce with no surplus liquid. As with conventional cooking they need to be well stirred from time to time, particularly towards the end of the cooking time. Pour into hot, sterilised jars, cover with acid-proof lids – plastic-coated or card-lined metal – or Porosan tied tightly over. Label them and store in a cool dark place. Allow to mature for at least two months before eating.

See recipes on pages 184–5.

• COD •

White fish is excellent when microwaved – moist, tender and full of flavour. Quite the best way to cook fish; though timing is critical as overcooking will toughen and harden it. If you like, a little lemon juice or butter can be added for flavour though the fish will cook quite happily in its own moisture.

Cod is best skinned so, if it has not already been done, here is the way to do it. Place the cod skin side down on your work surface. Dip your fingers in salt and grip the tail end firmly. With a sharp knife held horizontally, cut with a sawing motion between the flesh and the skin keeping as close to the skin as possible. Cut into portions if necessary.

TO COOK Arrange 450 g/1 lb fillets in a shallow dish with the thickest parts to the outside, thinner parts to the centre. They can overlap if necessary. Cover with cling film (plastic wrap), leaving a small gap for the steam to escape. Cook on full power for 3–4 minutes. At this stage the fish should just flake. Stand for 2 minutes when it will continue to cook and check again. By now the flesh should be opaque and flake easily. If it is still spongy, microwave a little longer. Season and serve or use for fish pies, fish cakes etc.

• CUTLETS AND STEAKS •

Arrange these in a dish with the thinner parts towards the centre. Cover and cook as the fillets, rearranging and turning over during the cooking. These thicker cuts may take a little longer to cook but check in the same way as above.

• COOKIES •

See BISCUITS.

• CORN-ON-THE-COB •

See SWEETCORN.

• COURGETTES (ZUCCHINI) •

These retain their delicate flavour and fresh colour beautifully and cook to a tender crispness in the microwave without ever becoming too soft. Choose straight firm courgettes with bright unwrinkled skins. Trim both ends and wash them. Cook whole if tiny, slice or halve and quarter them if larger.

TO COOK Place 450 g/1 lb sliced courgettes in a dish. The water that clings to them from washing is sufficient. Cover with cling film (plasic wrap), leaving a small gap for the steam to escape, and cook on full power for 8–12 minutes. Stand for 3 minutes. Keep slightly undercooked if using to top dishes like moussaka which will have further cooking. If serving as a vegetable, drain and toss in a little butter, season with salt and pepper.

COURGETTES WITH TOMATOES

Put 1 tablespoon oil and 1 finely chopped, small onion in a dish and cook on full power for 2–3 minutes until the onion has softened. Cut 450 g/1 lb medium courgettes into halves, then quarters lengthways and finally into 5–7.5-cm/2–3-in pieces. Add to the dish with the contents of 1 (227-g/8-oz) can/1 cup canned tomatoes. Season with a little salt and pepper, stir and cover with cling film (plastic wrap), leaving a small gap for the steam to escape. Cook on full power for 9–11 minutes, stirring half-way through the cooking. Stand for 3 minutes.

• CRANBERRIES •

These berries are crimson in colour with a sharp and slightly bitter flavour. They make an excellent sauce traditionally served with turkey but good, too, with game. The sauce can also be used as a pie filling or to top a cheesecake.

• CUSTARD •

Making a custard sauce in the microwave is so quick and simple that once tried you'll never do it any other way. Just remember to choose a jug (pitcher) – a glass one for preference so you can see what is happening – with sufficient room for the custard to rise during cooking. Once it reaches boiling point, it can be up and over the top in seconds!

TO COOK Measure 1 tablespoon each of custard powder (Bird's English dessert mix) and sugar into a jug (pitcher) and gradually blend in 300 ml/½ pint/1¼ cups milk until it it quite smooth. Cook on full power for 4 minutes, stirring after 1½ minutes and again at 3 minutes. Watch and remove as it starts boiling and rising up in the jug (pitcher). It will have thickened and be ready to use.

• CHOCOLATE CUSTARD •

Mix 1 tablespoon (unsweetened) cocoa powder with the custard powder and sugar.

• EGG CUSTARD SAUCE •

Measure 300 ml/½ pint/1¼ cups milk into a jug (pitcher) and heat on full power for 3 minutes, or until just boiling. Lightly whisk together 2 eggs and 25 g/1 oz/2 tablespoons sugar. Add a few drops of vanilla essence, if liked. Stir in the warmed milk, mix well and strain back into the jug. Stand the jug in a water-bath of warm water and cook for 4 minutes, stirring every minute. The custard should lightly coat the back of a spoon when cooked.

• EGG CUSTARDS •

Made in the microwave these are beautifully soft and creamy but if cooked too long or too fast, they will curdle in the same way as they do when conventionally baked. If your cooker has variable power, check in your handbook and follow the manufacturers' recommendations for this type of cooking. Cooking on full power works well if you stand the dish or dishes in an outer container of water (the water-bath method in conventional cooking). In this way, the water absorbs some of the microwaves and slows down the cooking.

INDIVIDUAL CUSTARDS Measure 300 ml/½ pint/1¼ cups milk into a jug (pitcher) and heat on full power for 2 minutes. Beat together 2 eggs and 25 g/1 oz/2 tablespoons sugar and stir in the warmed milk. Strain into four ramekin dishes (custard cups) and place in a water-bath. Arrange in a circle in the microwave and cook on full power for 4 minutes, turning the dishes once. The custard will be quite soft – the centre semi-liquid. Stand for 5 minutes and the centre should be firming. Leave to cool when it will continue to thicken. Chill and serve.

LARGE CUSTARD Pour 450 ml/$\frac{3}{4}$ pint/2 cups milk into a jug (pitcher) and heat on full power for 6 minutes. Whisk together 3 eggs and 50 g/2 oz/$\frac{1}{4}$ cup sugar. Stir in the milk and strain into a 750-ml/1$\frac{1}{4}$-pint soufflé dish. Stand this in a larger dish and pour in enough hot water to come well up the sides of the dish of custard. Cook on full power for 4 minutes. The mixture will still be soft but will firm up as it cools.

Both the custards cooked as above are smooth and creamy but the individual dishes have a firmer set.

• DESSERTS •

See PUDDINGS.

• DRIED BEANS •

See PULSES.

• DRIED FRUITS •

All dried fruits except for moisturised apricots and prunes need soaking to plump them. With a microwave this can be done by standing them half-way through the cooking rather than for hours prior to cooking. The fruit is tender and richly flavoured though not quite as soft as when pre-soaked and conventionally stewed. Pears and peaches in particular remain quite firm and if microwaving either of these fruits on their own, pre-soaking is recommended.

TO COOK 225 G / 8 OZ MIXED DRIED FRUIT Wash and drain the fruits and turn into a deep dish with 600 ml/1 pint/$2\frac{1}{2}$ cups water, cold tea or fruit juice. Cover with cling film (plastic wrap), leaving a small gap for the steam to escape, and cook on full power for 10 minutes, stirring once. Stand, covered, for 30 minutes. Cook on full power for a further 15 minutes, stirring once. Stir in 50 g/2 oz/$\frac{1}{4}$ cup sugar or to taste and stand for 5 minutes.

TO COOK 225 G / 8 OZ MOISTURISED APRICOTS OR PRUNES Turn the fruit into a dish and add 300 ml/$\frac{1}{2}$ pint/$1\frac{1}{4}$ cups water, cold tea or fruit juice. Cover with cling film (plastic wrap), leaving a small gap for the steam to escape, and cook on full power for 15 minutes, stirring once or twice. Stir in 50 g/2 oz/$\frac{1}{4}$ cup sugar or to taste and stand for 5 minutes.

• DUCK •

This can be cooked in the microwave and, like all poultry, the flesh will be moist and tender but the skin will be soft and pale. For a perfectly roasted duck microwave it until almost cooked, then transfer it to the conventional oven to brown and crisp the skin.

To prepare the duck, remove the giblets, rinse inside and wipe dry. Truss it to keep it a good shape. Duck is a fatty bird so the skin should be pricked to allow the fat to run out.

TIMING about 7–9 minutes per 450 g/1 lb.

TO COOK Put a 1.75-kg/4-lb prepared duck on a roasting rack over a dish, breast side down. Cover with greaseproof (waxed) paper or a slit roasting bag so the fat does not spatter all over the cooker and cook on full power for 10 minutes. Drain off any fat. Turn the duck breast side up, cover and cook for a further 18 minutes on full power. Have the oven heated to hot (230 C, 450 F, gas 8). Transfer the duck to a roasting tin (pan), spoon over a little of the fatty juices and roast for about 15 minutes until brown and crisp.

A sharp apple sauce is a good accompaniment to the rich meat of the duck and you can make it while the duck finishes roasting.

Core 2 cooking (green) apples (about 225 g/8 oz each) and score round the centre. Put into a dish – do not add any water – cover with cling film (plastic wrap), leaving a small gap for the steam to escape, and cook on full power for 4–6 minutes. It does not matter if they overcook slightly until they collapse. Discard the top halves of the skins and fork the softened apple into a dish. Stir in 1 tablespoon sugar and 15 g/$\frac{1}{2}$ oz/1 tablespoon butter. Beat until smooth. Taste to see if it needs a little more sugar, but keep it quite sharp.

• DUCK PIECES •

Leg joints, wings and breast fillets are now widely available and can be cooked in the microwave. A crisp skin does, however, add considerably not only to their appearance but also their flavour, so after cooking in the microwave crisp the skin under the grill (broiler).

TO COOK Place 4 duck pieces (275–350 g/10–12 oz each) skin side down on a roasting rack over a dish. Cover with greaseproof (waxed) paper and cook on full power for 10 minutes. Drain off fat and juices. Turn skin side up and cook on full power for 10 minutes. Stand for 5 minutes, then grill (broil) until crisp and brown.

• EGGPLANTS •

See AUBERGINES.

• EGGS •

Eggs can be cooked in the microwave in various ways but because they cook so quickly, it is not always easy to get them just right. When poached or baked there will doubtless be occasions when you find a little of the white is undercooked. Nevertheless try to get used to the idea of removing the eggs before the whites are quite ready as they continue cooking during the short standing time Longer cooking will only harden the yolks.

The following guidelines will help you to get the best results.

◇ In conventional cooking the white cooks first. In the microwave it is just the reverse. The yolks cook faster than the whites because of their higher fat content which attracts more microwave energy. So watch them carefully and remove before the whites are completely cooked.

◇ Always pierce the yolk with the tip of a kitchen knife or a cocktail stick (toothpick) to puncture the membrane. Otherwise it is likely to burst.

◇ Do not cook eggs in their shells. They will explode! So forget boiled eggs but try poached, baked and scrambled instead.

• TO POACH EGGS •

Bring 150 ml/¼ pint/⅔ cup water with a pinch of salt to the boil in a dish. Crack an egg into a saucer, pierce the yolk and slide it into the water. Cover and cook for 45–60 seconds. Stand for 1 minute. Lift out with a slotted spoon to drain.
2 eggs will take 1–1½ minutes   3 eggs will take 2–2½ minutes
4 eggs will take 2½–3 minutes

• TO BAKE EGGS •

Lightly grease a ramekin dish (custard cup). Break in an egg and pierce the yolk. Add a tablespoon of cream if you like, then cover with cling film (plastic wrap). Bake on full power for 1 minute. Stand for 1 minute.
2 eggs will take 1–1¼ minutes   3 eggs will take 1½–1¾ minutes
4 eggs will take 1¾–2 minutes.

• TO SCRAMBLE EGGS •

Beat 2 eggs with 2 tablespoons milk or water, season lightly with salt and pepper. Add 1 tablespoon butter and cook on full power for 1½–2 minutes. As you see the outer edge begin to rise and become firm, take the dish out and give a good stir, incorporating the cooked parts with the still liquid areas. Continue to cook for the remaining 1–2 minutes but remove the eggs while still moist and fork them through. You will soon learn to judge just when to remove the dish so the eggs are cooked to your liking.
4 eggs will take 2½–3 minutes
6 eggs will take 3½–4 minutes

• FENNEL •

As Florence fennel grows, the leaf stalk swells at the base to give a bulbous 'head'. These layers of crisp and white swollen stalks have a mild aniseed flavour. They can be eaten raw in salads or cooked and served as a hot vegetable. Fennel is particularly good with poultry and fish.

Prepare the fennel by removing any stringy or tough outer layers. Trim the base and cut off any hard round stalks, then slice across thinly.

To cook Put 225 g/8 oz sliced fennel in a dish with 3 tablespoons water. Cover with cling film (plastic wrap), leaving a small gap for the steam to escape, and cook on full power for 4–5 minutes. Drain, season and serve.

• FISH AND SHELLFISH •

All fish you conventionally poach or steam will benefit from being cooked in the microwave. The quick cooking ensures firm, moist flesh with no loss of the delicate flavour.

Fish will cook in its own moisture though lemon juice, butter or wine can be used to add their distinctive flavours.

When cooking fillets arrange them in a dish, thinner parts to the centre, tucked under or slightly overlapped to give as even a thickness as possible. Cover with cling film (plastic wrap) and cook for the recommended time which is usually 4–5 minutes for 450 g/1 lb. Rearrange the fillets half-way through cooking.

Timing is critical because overcooking will destroy the delicate flavour and make the flesh tough and chewy. Microwave for the minimum time, then check. If the thinner parts are opaque and the flesh flakes easily, let the fish stand for 3 minutes, by which time the thicker parts should have lost their translucency, be creamy white and flake easily.

Whole fish needs its skin slashed in two or three places so it does not burst. Turn the fish over half-way through cooking and cover the head and tail with small pieces of foil as soon as they are cooked or they will become brittle.

Fish can be cooked in a roasting bag, wrapped in greaseproof (waxed) paper or laid in a dish and covered with cling film (plastic wrap). Very large fish like salmon can be curved to fit into a round dish. Once cooked the fish will remain curved. Again timing is critical and the flesh should flake easily when tested with a fork.

Fish coated with egg and breadcrumbs can be cooked in a little hot oil but needs a browning dish to crisp it. Fish in batter that needs deep frying must not be attempted. The temperature cannot be controlled and there is a danger of fire.

Shellfish can also be cooked in the microwave but needs very careful timing. Overcooking will toughen the flesh and with shellfish often being quite expensive to buy, this would be a disaster.

See individual fish and shellfish for full cooking instructions.

• FRENCH FRIES •

See POTATOES.

• FRUIT •

Fruit cooked in the microwave has a much fuller flavour and richer colour than when cooked conventionally. Because it cooks so rapidly and needs the minimum of water, the flavour is not diluted or the colour destroyed. This quick cooking does, however, mean that the skins of some fruits don't have time to soften. Plum skins in particular can be disagreeably tough and you may prefer the longer conventional cooking to soften them.

Apples need scoring so they don't burst during cooking. In fact any fruit with a firm skin – for example, apricots, gooseberries or blackcurrants – is likely to burst. It is sometimes recommended that the skins are pricked to avoid this but this is unnecessary. Cover the dish to contain any spattering.

Whole firm fruits, such as apricots, cherries, peaches, nectarines and pears, respond well to poaching in a sugar syrup. This can be made with water, wine or fruit juice and you will find instructions under the individual fruits.

• GAME BIRDS •

Young game birds can be cooked in the microwave; older, tougher ones are best casseroled conventionally. Don't overcook or the rather dry flesh will toughen and don't expect them to colour as appetisingly as a conventionally roasted bird.

The flesh needs a little fat to prevent it drying out so spread the breasts with butter or slices of bacon. Remember to use wooden cocktail sticks (toothpicks) or skewers – not metal ones – when trussing. Cooking in a roasting bag will help to keep the flesh moist.

If you are not satisfied with the colour, remove any bacon rashers and let the birds have their standing time in a hot oven (220C, 425F, gas 7) to brown and crisp the skin.

• GAMMON (HAM) •

Gammon joints (ham slabs) can be cooked in the same way as bacon joints (slabs) (see page 45) allowing 8–9 minutes per 450 g/1 lb. On the whole, conventional cooking in water produces a more evenly cooked and softer-textured meat.

Check with your supplier whether the piece needs soaking and be guided by his recommendations. This can either be done by soaking in cold water for several hours or, more rapidly, by putting in a pan of water and bringing to the boil on the hob. Drain off the water and run cold water over the meat to cool it. Drain and pat dry, then microwave.

For large pieces gentler cooking produces the best results, allowing the centre to cook without hardening the outer edges. Use the power recommended by the manufacturers of your cooker. If you don't have variable power, cook on full power for half the calculated cooking time. Stand the meat for 20–30 minutes tented with foil, then finish cooking.

If the piece is unevenly shaped, don't forget to wrap the thinner end in foil half-way through the cooking.

• GAMMON (HAM) STEAKS •

These cook well with a moister finish than when conventionally grilled or fried (broiled or pan-fried). Remove the rind and snip the fat at intervals so the meat doesn't curl during cooking.

TO COOK A 100 G/4 OZ GAMMON (HAM) STEAK Place on a dish and cover with greaseproof (waxed) paper, cook on full power for 2–2½ minutes. Stand for 2 minutes.
2 (100-g/4-oz) gammon steaks will take 4–4½ minutes
4 (100-g/4-oz) gammon steaks will take 6–7 minutes

TO SERVE WITH PINEAPPLE Put a slice of canned pineapple on the cooked gammon, spoon over a little of the juice and cook on full power for 1 minute.

• GARLIC BREAD •

If you are used to heating garlic bread conventionally, the softness of the microwaved version may disappoint you. It tastes good but it lacks the familiar crunchy crust of oven-baked or reheated French bread. It is not possible to get a crisp outside with a soft inside in the microwave. It is either all soft or all crisp.

Here is the crisp-all-through version. Put 50 g/2 oz/¼ cup salted butter in a small dish and work into it 1–2 crushed garlic cloves or about 2-cm/¾-in garlic purée. Heat on full power for 1–1½ minutes until melted. Cut a small French loaf or half a baguette into 12 (1-cm/½-in) thick slices. Brush 6 slices all over on both sides with melted butter and arrange on a roasting rack. Cook on full power for 2 minutes, when the bread should feel firm to the touch. Transfer to a wire rack to cool and crisp. Repeat with the remaining slices. Serve with pâtés, soups and salads.

• GOOSE •

This is a large bird with a size range of between 3.25 kg/7 lb and 6.75 kg/15 lb. It can be microwaved, though not all cookers will accommodate its length of body, particularly those with turntables.

If your microwave is large enough, cook it in the same way as duck (see page 66) allowing about 7 minutes per 450 g/1 lb.

Make sure you have a young goose or it will be tough. Deep yellow fat is the sign of an old bird.

• GOOSEBERRIES •

Gooseberries cook quickly and well in the microwave though the skins tend to be a little tougher than when conventionally cooked.

Wash the gooseberries and top and tail them (snip off both ends), though this is not necessary if you are going to sieve them.

TO COOK Spread out 450 g/1 lb prepared gooseberries in a shallow dish with 2 tablespoons water and 100 g/4 oz/½ cup sugar. Cover with cling film (plastic wrap), leaving a small gap for the steam to escape, and cook on full power for 4–5 minutes. Serve hot or cold.

TO PURÉE Cook for a further 2–3 minutes until the fruit softens completely and collapses. Rub through a sieve to a smooth purée.

GOOSEBERRY FOOL (CREAM)

When the purée is cold, marble through it 150 ml/¼ pint/⅔ cup lightly whipped double (heavy) cream. It looks more attractive if it isn't blended in completely. Spoon into wine glasses and serve with sponge fingers (Ladyfingers).

GOOSEBERRY ICE CREAM

Make the above mixture, blending the cream and purée smoothly together. Freeze. When the mixture begins to set, beat it well and return to the freezer.

• GRAPEFRUIT •

These large citrus fruits can have either yellow or pink flesh, the pink being the sweeter. Usually segmented and eaten raw on their own or added to sweet and savoury salads, they can also be halved and served hot.

Ginger Grapefruit

Cut 2 grapefruit in half and, using a serrated grapefruit knife, cut between the membrane of each segment releasing them from the pith. Sprinkle over the halves 2 tablespoons ginger wine, 50 g/2 oz/$\frac{1}{4}$ cup demerara sugar and 25 g/1 oz/1 tablespoon finely chopped preserved ginger, dividing it equally between them.

Place the grapefruit halves in a shallow dish and cook on full power for 3 minutes, turning the grapefruit around after 2 minutes. Serve hot, garnished with sprigs of mint.

• GREENGAGES •

These can be cooked in the microwave but expect the skins to be tougher than when stewed conventionally. Choose firm ripe fruit. Wash if necessary and remove any stalks. They can be cooked whole – pricking them helps prevent the skin bursting but this is not essential – or halved and stoned (pitted). They are also very good when poached whole in a sugar syrup. Cook in the same way as apricots (see page 40).

• GROUSE •

Young birds are the ones for cooking in the microwave and a plump bird should serve two. Cook in the same way as pheasant (see page 97).

See also GAME BIRDS.

• GUINEA FOWL •

Although guinea fowl is now a domesticated bird farmed like poultry, it has a slightly gamey flavour. The flesh is on the dry side and needs a covering of fat. Cook in the same way as pheasant (see page 97).

See also GAME BIRDS.

• HADDOCK •

A firm, white-fleshed fish similar in shape to cod but with a finer flavour. It is usually cut into fillets and is cooked in the same way as cod (see page 62). Smoked haddock is similarly cooked with the addition of a little butter.

See also FISH.

• HAKE •

This fish has close white flesh and is similar to cod. Cook it in the same way as cod (see page 62).

• HALIBUT •

This is a large, flattish fish with richly-flavoured, firm white flesh. Smaller ones are sold whole, larger ones cut into steaks. Serve it hot with lemon juice or cold, flaked, with mayonnaise. Cook in the same way as cod (see page 62).

See also FISH.

• HAM •

See GAMMON.

• HARE •

Young hares can be roasted, older animals need to be jugged (cooked in an earthenware pot or jug) for anything up to 3 hours to tenderise them and this is best done conventionally over a low heat.

• HARICOT BEANS •

See PULSES and CHICK PEAS.

• HEARTS •

These can be very tough unless they have long, slow cooking which is best done conventionally.

• HERRINGS •

Fresh herrings should have a shine to their skins and feel fairly stiff. They cook well in the microwave though it you like a crisp skin, they will need to be conventionally grilled or fried (broiled or sautéed).

Cut and clean (eviscerate) them and remove the heads if you wish. Score the skin two or three times with a sharp knife.

TO COOK Arrange 4 medium herrings head to tail in an oblong shallow dish. Cover with greaseproof (waxed) paper and cook on full power for 5–6 minutes, turning over and rearranging half-way through the cooking. Stand for 3 minutes. Remember they continue to cook during standing time after which the flesh should flake easily. If not, cook a little longer. Serve with Dijon mustard.

TO BONE If you are sousing herrings, they will need to be boned. To do this, slit along the belly and clean it out. Turn the fish flesh side down on to a board and press firmly all along the backbone with the heel of your hand. Turn the fish over and peel off the backbone, taking with it the little bones.

SOUSED HERRINGS

Prepare 4 medium herrings as above. If the fillets are very large, cut them lengthways in two. Roll each piece up from head end to tail, skin side out. Secure with a wooden cocktail stick (toothpick) and arrange round the outer edge of a shallow dish. Add a bay leaf and a few parsley stalks to the dish. Peel and thinly slice an onion into rings and distribute over the dish.

Put 1 teaspoon sugar and ½ teaspoon salt into a measuring jug and pour on 4 tablespoons boiling water. Stir to dissolve sugar and salt, then stir in 150 ml/¼ pint/⅔ cup cider vinegar and 2 teaspoons pickling spice (whole mixed spices). Pour over the herrings and cover with cling film (plastic wrap), leaving a small gap for the steam to escape. Cook on full power for 8–10 minutes. Turn the dish twice if you don't have a turntable. Leave to cool, covered. Refrigerate before serving.

• JAM (PRESERVES) •

Microwaving is the ideal way of cooking small quantities of jam. The colour and flavour is excellent and with no direct heat it will not stick and is unlikely to burn. Fruits with a high pectin content will set most easily; these include blackcurrants, redcurrants, apples and gooseberries. Raspberries, cherries and strawberries are medium to low in pectin. They will need some help to achieve a good set in the form of lemon juice or bottled pectin.

The skins of fruits like plums do not soften so well in the microwave and you may not find them to your liking. Check before stirring in the sugar because after that has been added, they will not soften any further.

As in conventional jam-making the fruit must be cooked until soft before the sugar is added. Make sure the bowl you are using is sufficiently large for the fruit to boil up but not over and use oven gloves when moving the bowl because it will become extremely hot.

Once the sugar has been stirred in and has dissolved, the jam is boiled rapidly to setting point, stirring it occasionally. Test for setting by putting a little on a saucer. When cold it should wrinkle when pushed gently with your finger. Pot in hot sterilised jars in the usual way.

• TO STERILISE JARS •

Quarter fill clean jars with water and bring to a full boil in the microwave. As the water in each jar boils remove the jar from the microwave. Empty out the water and turn upside down on absorbent kitchen paper.

See also Preserves section on pages 184–7.

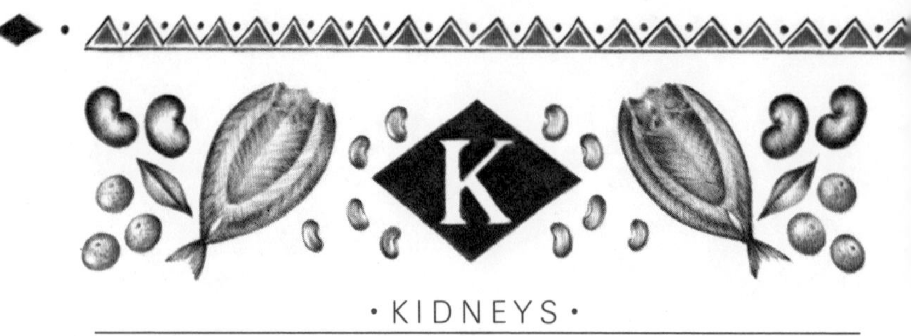

• KIDNEYS •

Lambs' kidneys are deliciously moist and tender when cooked in the microwave.

TO PREPARE Cut in half and pull off the membrane. With a pair of scissors snip out the white cores. Wash and dry the kidneys on absorbent kitchen paper.

TO COOK Put 25 g/1 oz/2 tablespoons butter in a dish and heat on full power until melted, about 1 minute. Add 450 g/1 lb kidneys, turning them over in the butter, cover with cling film (plastic wrap), leaving a small gap for the steam to escape, and cook on full power for 2 minutes. Stir, moving those round the outer edge into the centre. Cover and cook for a further 3–4 minutes. Stand for 3 minutes. They should be just tinged with pink in the centre when cooked. Season with salt and pepper and serve on toast. Alternatively, stir a little thick (heavy) cream into the juices before seasoning and serving with rice.

• KIPPERS •

These are herrings that have been split, gutted (eviscerated), lightly salted and smoked. Cooking time is short whichever method you use but in the microwave the smell is contained and the fish can be cooked on the serving plate. Timing is about 4 minutes per 450 g/1 lb.

TO COOK Place a pair of kippers (about 175 g/6 oz each) skin side down on a large plate. Cover with cling film (plastic wrap), pierce and cook on full power for 2 minutes. Rearrange the kippers and cook for a further 1 minute.

• KOHLRABI •

This is a member of the cabbage family but is grown for its swollen base stem, where all the nourishment is stored, rather than its leaves. The skin can be white, green or purple and its shape and flavour is rather like that of a turnip.

Choose small, firm kohlrabi, about 5 cm/2 in across. Larger ones are likely to be tough. The leaves will have been removed so all you need to do is to trim it top and bottom and peel (pare) it. It can be grated or sliced and served raw in salads, or cooked in the same way as celeriac or turnip.

TO COOK Slice 450 g/1 lb prepared kohlrabi into a dish and add 2 tablespoons water. Cover with cling film (plastic wrap), leaving a small gap for the steam to escape, and cook on full power for 8–10 minutes, stirring once. Drain, season and serve.

• KUMQUATS •

These small citrus fruits with their bitter-sweet taste look like tiny oranges. They are usually candied or preserved in sugar syrup but sliced and cooked in orange juice make a lovely sauce for ice cream.

KUMQUAT SAUCE

Put 150 ml/$\frac{1}{4}$ pint/$\frac{2}{3}$ cup orange juice, freshly squeezed for preference, into a dish with 25 g/1 oz/2 tablespoons sugar and 1 teaspoon arrowroot. Cook on full power for 4 minutes, stirring twice.

Wash and dry 100 g/4 oz kumquats. Cut each crosswise into 3 or 4 slices and remove the pips with the point of a knife. Stir the prepared fruit into the orange syrup, cover with cling film (plastic wrap), leaving a small gap for the steam to escape, and cook on full power for 3 minutes, stirring once. Chill and serve with vanilla ice cream.

The skins will be firm, but tender, their bitterness softened by the orange syrup. A tablespoon of Cointreau may be stirred in before serving.

• LADY'S FINGERS •

See OKRA.

• LAMB •

All the cuts of lamb which you roast conventionally – shoulder, leg and even crown roast – can be cooked in the microwave. The more even the shape, the more even the cooking, so it is a good idea to have the meat boned and rolled where possible. If you would rather cook your meat on the bone, then remember to cover the thinner ends with foil half-way through the cooking.

Timing will be 7–9 minutes per 450 g/1 lb depending on whether you like your meat medium or well-done. The safest way to judge this is by using a thermometer. This must be a microwave thermometer if you are leaving it in the meat in the cooker. A chart of temperatures comes with these special thermometers so you know exactly what to aim for.

Although some colouring occurs in the microwave, the meat will not look anything like a conventionally roasted one. Colourants can be brushed on but they don't produce crispness. The only way to achieve this is to finish cooking in a hot oven.

• ROAST LAMB •

Put a 1.75-kg/4-lb shoulder of lamb fat side down on a roasting rack, cover with a slit roasting bag and cook on full power for 10 minutes. Turn the meat over and drain off any juices. Re-cover and cook for a further 15 minutes. Transfer the joint to a roasting tin (pan), baste with a spoonful or two of the fatty juices, season with salt and pepper and continue cooking in a hot oven (220 C, 425 F, gas 7) for 20–30 minutes until well browned and cooked through. This timing gives you well-cooked lamb.

• CHOPS AND LEG STEAKS •

These are sufficiently tender to cook in the microwave though they will lack colour. If they are to be cooked in a sauce, it is not so important, but if they are to be served plain, they look more appetising with a little more colour. Use a browning dish or the grill (broiler) to provide this.

• MINCED/GROUND LAMB •

This cooks well and is the basis for a whole range of dishes that can be cooked most successfully in the microwave.

• LAMB STEW •

Use lamb fillet trimmed of surplus fat for stews. It is a tender cut and cooks well this way. If you are feeling thoroughly lazy, just put 450 g/1 lb cubed lamb fillet into a dish. Stir in 1 (300-g/10.6-oz) can country vegetable soup (300 ml/½ pint/1¼ cups is the quantity you need). Cover with cling film (plastic wrap), leaving a small gap for the steam to escape, and cook on full power for 20 minutes, stirring twice. Stand for 5 minutes and serve. Quick and tasty.

See also MEAT.

• LEEKS •

Leeks are often cooked conventionally in too much water and end up soggy and limp. In the microwave they need only a spoonful or two of water so they retain their colour and flavour and have a pleasantly firm texture. Choose straight white leeks with fresh green tops. Any with yellowed tops and a bulbous base could well be tough. Trim away the roots and most of the green top. Turn upside down in a jug (pitcher) or bowl of cold water and leave to soak. This way any grit will float out.

TO COOK SLICED LEEKS Put 450 g/1 lb leeks cut into 2.5-cm/1-in slices in a dish with 2 tablespoons water. Cover with cling film (plastic wrap), leaving a small gap for the steam to escape, and cook on full power for 7–9 minutes, stirring half-way through the cooking. Drain, season and serve.

TO COOK WHOLE LEEKS Arrange 450 g/1 lb whole leeks in a dish with 2 tablespoons water. Cover with cling film (plastic wrap), leaving a small gap for the steam to escape, and cook on full power for 7–9 minutes, rearranging the leeks half-way through the cooking. Drain and serve. Keep them on the firm side if you want to cook them further – wrapped in ham in a cheese sauce, for example.

• LENTILS •

These cook very well in the microwave and unlike most pulses need no soaking.

CURRIED LENTILS Put 25 g/1 oz/1 tablespoon butter in a dish with a finely chopped medium onion and a crushed garlic clove. Cover with cling film (plastic wrap), leaving a small gap for the steam to escape, and cook on full power for 2 minutes. Wash 75 g/3 oz red lentils, drain and add them to the dish. Stir in 1 tablespoon curry powder and cook for 3 minutes. Stir in 600 ml/1 pint/2½ cups boiling water, cover and cook for 25 minutes.

• LIVER •

This can be moist and delicious cooked in the microwave but be careful over the timing because it becomes hard and grainy if overdone.

Calf's liver is the most expensive; delicately flavoured and meltingly tender, it needs only the briefest of cooking. Lamb's liver is more readily available with a slightly stronger flavour but can be delicious when carefully cooked. Pig's liver is much stronger in flavour with a soft texture and is best for pâtés. Ox liver has a coarse texture but is very good after long slow cooking, best done conventionally.

LIVER AND BACON

Halve 4 rashers (slices) of rindless streaky bacon. Put in a dish and cook on full power for 1½ minutes. Remove the bacon and set aside. Add 1 tablespoon oil to the dish together with 1 finely chopped medium onion and cook on full power for 2 minutes until soft. Wash and dry 450 g/1 lb thinly sliced lamb's liver. Sprinkle it with 1 tablespoon flour, add to the dish and cook, covered, on full power for 1½ minutes. Arrange the bacon over the liver and pour on 150 ml/¼ pint/⅔ cup hot beef stock or gravy. Cover and cook for 3 minutes. Serve.

• LOBSTER •

Lobster can be cooked in the microwave and, admittedly based on limited testing, it tastes just as good as when conventionally cooked in boiling salted water. The lobster must be killed first by driving the point of a sharp knife through the natural cross on the head under which the brain lies. Death is instantaneous.

TO COOK Put a 450 g/1 lb lobster in a dish with 6 tablespoons water and cook on full power for 7–8 minutes. It will gradually change from blue-black to red starting with the legs and claws. When the colour change is complete, it should be cooked. It will not turn as bright red as boiled lobster and there may be the odd patches of dark shell on the claws, but don't overcook or the flesh will toughen.

When cold put the point of a strong chopping knife down through the cross on top of the head and bring the blade down through the tail to divide it in two. Turn the lobster and divide the rest of the head in the same way. Remove the bag in the head which is inedible and also the thin black line running through the tail meat. The green, creamy part is the liver and is perfectly good to eat. Lift out the tail meat, cut into slanting slices and return to the shell. Crack the claws. You can remove the meat and put it into the head shells or leave it in the claws and arrange them with the rest of the lobster on a dish. Serve with mayonnaise.

• MACKEREL •

This is a round, oily fish with blue-black markings and a creamy flesh. It can be cooked in the same way as herring including sousing (see page 76). When microwaved the flavour of the flesh is very good but the skin looks uncooked. If you like a crisp, brown skin, you will be happier with conventional grilling (broiling).

The fishmonger will clean the fish for you and cut the head off if you wish. To clean the fish yourself, just slit along the belly, remove the entrails (eviscerate) and wash thoroughly.

TO COOK Arrange 4 medium mackerel (about 225 g/8 oz each) in a dish alternating head to tail. Add 2 tablespoons water, cover with cling film (plastic wrap), leaving a small gap for the steam to escape, and cook on full power for 8 minutes, turning and rearranging half-way through the cooking. Stand for 3 minutes. If cooked the flesh should flake easily with a fork.

A sharp sauce made with gooseberries goes well with the oily flesh of the mackerel.

Gooseberry Sauce

Wash 225 g/8 oz green gooseberries and put in a dish with 1 tablespoon water. Cover with cling film (plastic wrap), leaving a small gap for the steam to escape, and cook on full power for 4–5 minutes until well softened. Sieve to a purée and stir in 1 tablespoon sugar and a knob of butter.

• MANGE-TOUT (SNOW) PEAS •

As the name implies you eat the whole vegetable pod and peas. The pods should be bright green and flat with tiny peas just apparent under the skin. Wash if necessary. Top and tail them, then trim the ends pulling the strings away from the edges as you do so.

To cook Put 350 g/12 oz prepared mange-tout peas in a dish with 2 tablespoons water. Cover with cling film (plastic wrap), leaving a small gap for the steam to escape, and cook on full power for 5–6 minutes. Stand for 2 minutes, drain and season. They should be crisp and fresh-tasting, never soft.

• MARMALADE •

It is possible to make small quantities of marmalade in the microwave but only the jelly type containing thin strips (shreds) of peel is really successful. The chunks of peel required in thicker marmalade just don't soften and are unpleasant to eat.

Use either one type of citrus fruit or a combination and cook until the peel is tender before adding any sugar.

Use an ovenproof glass bowl and make sure it is large enough to contain the bubbling marmalade. Remember that the bowl will get very hot so use oven gloves or a cloth when touching it.

After the recommended boiling time check if the marmalade will set by spooning a little into a saucer. Leave it until cold, then push it with the side of your little finger. If it wrinkles, setting point is reached. Pot and seal in the usual way.

See also recipe for Three Fruits Marmalade on page 187.

• MARROW (SQUASH OR LARGE • ZUCCHINI)

Avoid very large marrows as they are likely to be fibrous in texture and insipid in flavour. When boiled conventionally, they can be watery and tasteless. When cooked in the microwave without water they have a firmer texture and much better flavour. When halved and stuffed, they cook in a fraction of the time they take to bake in the conventional oven.

Peel (pare) and trim off the ends, halve and remove the seeds. If the marrow is to be cooked plainly, cut into small cubes.

TO COOK Place 450 g/1 lb cubed marrow in a dish, cover with cling film (plastic wrap), leaving a small gap for the steam to escape, and cook on full power for 6–9 minutes, stirring half-way through the cooking. Drain, toss in butter, season and serve.

Cubed marrow can also be cooked like the Courgettes with Tomatoes (see page 63).

• MEAT •

There are a number of advantages to cooking large cuts of meat in the microwave. It will be quicker and cleaner; the meat will be moist with a good flavour and will generally shrink less. It will not, however, look like a conventional roast because it has been steamed. There is no dry heat to brown and crisp the outside. If you are cooking a large piece of meat over a longish period, some colouring occurs though the overall appearance tends more to beige than brown in both beef and lamb. Colouring can be applied in the form of specially prepared seasonings and browning agents and brushed-on liquids like a soy or brown sauce.

If these additions don't appeal, then microwave the meat until almost cooked and transfer it to a hot oven (220 C, 425 F, gas 7) to brown and crisp. Not an extravagance if you are already roasting potatoes and perhaps baking a fruit pie.

Cuts that are boned and rolled to an even shape cook the most evenly in the microwave. They should be tied with string or secured with wooden skewers to keep them in shape. If the shape is uneven, like a leg of lamb, then shield the thinner end with foil for half the cooking time or it will dry out and toughen.

Meat should be raised above its juices when cooking and this is most easily done by standing it on a roasting rack. Improvise if you like by resting the meat on one or two upturned saucers standing in a dish. The fats and juices need draining off during cooking as they attract microwave energy and slow down the cooking.

The meat doesn't have to be covered during cooking but as there is a certain amount of spattering, it makes sense to contain this by putting the meat in a roasting bag or a covered dish or covering it with greaseproof (waxed) paper.

All meat can be cooked on full power though you may find with some cuts a medium setting – and therefore slower cooking – produces more even and tender results. Some microwave cookers have an auto facility for roasting meats so there is no problem. If your cooker has variable power, follow the manufacturers' recommendations for cooking meat. A microwave thermometer takes the guesswork out of timing and ensures the meat is cooked to the correct temperature. It can be inserted in the meat towards the end of the cooking time, when the meat has had all its turnings. In no circumstances must an ordinary meat thermometer be used inside the microwave.

Once the meat is cooked, it has to have a standing time. It should be loosely covered with foil and left for 15–20 minutes. This standing time is important because, as you will see if you are using a microwave thermometer, the temperature continues to rise during this period and the cooking is completed.

If you are transferring the meat to the conventional oven for browning do so straight away – minus the thermometer. The standing time of 15 minutes or so then takes place in the hot oven.

• STEWS (CASSEROLES) •

Meat can be stewed (casseroled) in the microwave provided you use some of the leaner, tender cuts of meats like lamb, veal and pork. Stewing beef, even after marinating and cooking on low power, can be disappointing. The flavours don't develop and mingle in the same way as they do in long, slow conventional cooking and the meat is not so tender.

• CHOPS (CUTLETS), STEAKS AND OTHER • SMALL CUTS OF MEAT

These will be tender and moist but lack the eye and palate appeal of grilled (broiled) or fried meat. This can be overcome by the use of a browning dish but by the time this has been heated and perhaps reheated, little time is saved over conventional frying or grilling (sautéeing or broiling).

• MINCED/GROUND BEEF •

This cooks extremely well. It is moist, pleasantly coloured and can be cooked and served in the same dish.

See also BEEF, LAMB, PORK, VEAL and VENISON.

• MERINGUES •

Whether or not you feel meringues are successful in the microwave depends on your expectations. You can't make the traditional meringues of whisked (beaten) egg white and sugar that bake to a crisp, lightly coloured shell with a hint of chewiness in the centre. You can make a modern version using firm fondant that will rise and crisp, be very white and close-textured. They can be sandwiched with cream or broken up and folded into cream mixtures, but they quickly soften so should be prepared only a short time before they are to be eaten.

Break up an egg white with a fork – don't whisk (beat) it up – and gradually work in up to 275g/10oz/2cups sifted icing (confectioners') sugar. Blend in the sugar a little at a time, working it in with the fork to start with, then with your fingers until you have a firm smooth fondant.

TO COOK Break off a small piece about the size of a cherry and shape it into a ball. Place six of these in a circle on greaseproof (waxed) paper on a plate, spacing them out well, and cook on full power for 1 minute. They should stay puffed up when you open the door. If not give them a few more seconds. Transfer to a wire rack and cook the next batch. Wrap any unused fondant in cling film (plastic wrap) to prevent it drying out. This quantity makes about 40 small meringues.

Note Do not try to use the bought ready-to-roll fondant – it just melts.

• MONKFISH •

Like all white fish, monkfish cooks extremely well in the microwave. It has a firm-textured flesh with a delicious flavour, often compared to that of lobster. When cooked the flesh flakes into chunky pieces. It is sold in fillets and all you need to do is pull off any stray pieces of membrane and wash the fish. It can be cooked quite simply like cod allowing 4 minutes per 450 g/1 lb and then served with a creamy sauce, a tomato sauce or a dish of ratatouille. If left until cold, flaked and mixed with mayonnaise, it makes a lovely summer salad.

Monkfish in Green Mayonnaise

Put 350 g/12 oz monkfish in a dish, cover with cling film (plastic wrap) and cook on full power for 3–4 minutes. Set aside to cool and make the mayonnaise. Put 2 egg yolks, 1 tablespoon lemon juice, 1 tablespoon each of chopped parsley and snipped (chopped) chives, salt and pepper into a liquidiser and blend for a few seconds. Remove the centre cap and slowly pour 300 ml/½ pint/1¼ cups oil on to the revolving blades, very gradually at first until the mixture thickens, then in a steady stream. Check seasoning.

Flake the cold monkfish into large chunks. Mix with the mayonnaise and serve on a bed of shredded lettuce.

• MULLET •

Grey mullet is silvery in colour with firm white flesh, not unlike bass. Red mullet is smaller, crimson in colour and belongs to a different family. It has a delicate and delicious flavour. The liver is a delicacy and should not be discarded with the rest of the innards.

Clean the fish (eviscerate) and scale it by using the blunt edge of a knife, scraping off the scales working from the tail to the head. Rinse the fish well in cold water. As with all round fish the skin should be slashed two or three times on each side before microwaving. Allow about 4 minutes per 450 g/1 lb, but test before the alloted time and, if the fish flakes easily, it is cooked.

• MUSHROOMS •

Whole or sliced these have a good texture and flavour cooked in the microwave. Choose fresh, firm mushrooms avoiding any that are beginning to brown or have wizened stalks. Never peel them (remove the skins), just wipe with a damp cloth. If they are very dirty, rinse them quickly in water but don't let them soak. Pat dry and trim the stalks (stems).

TO COOK Put 25 g/1 oz/2 tablespoons butter in a dish and heat on full power until melted, about 45 seconds. Turn 225 g/8 oz small mushrooms in the butter, cover with cling film (plastic wrap) and cook on full power for 3–4 minutes, stirring once. Stand for 1 minute. The same quantity of sliced mushrooms will take about the same time.

If after cooking you feel there's too much liquid – mushrooms exude quite a lot of moisture – drain it off into a small bowl and microwave on full power until it is reduced to a spoonful or two. Pour these concentrated juices over the mushrooms and serve.

• MUSSELS •

Like all live shellfish, mussels must be absolutely fresh and should be eaten on the day they are bought.

With a sharp knife, scrape off the barnacles and pull away the beard-like strands. Give them a good scrub in plenty of cold water and discard any with broken or cracked shells. You should also discard any open shells that don't close immediately when tapped.

TO COOK Put 300 ml/$\frac{1}{2}$ pint/$1\frac{1}{4}$ cups dry white wine in a large mixing bowl with a finely chopped onion, a crushed garlic clove and a seasoning of salt and freshly ground black pepper. Cover with cling film (plastic wrap), leaving a small gap for the steam to escape, and cook on full power for 5 minutes. Put in 1 kg/2 lb prepared mussels and cook for 4–5 minutes until they open. Transfer the mussels to a tureen or serving dish. Any that have not opened should be discarded.

Strain the liquor into a bowl. Whisk in 25 g/1 oz/2 tablespoons butter, check seasoning and heat for 2 minutes on full power. Pour over the mussels and sprinkle with chopped parsley. Serve immediately.

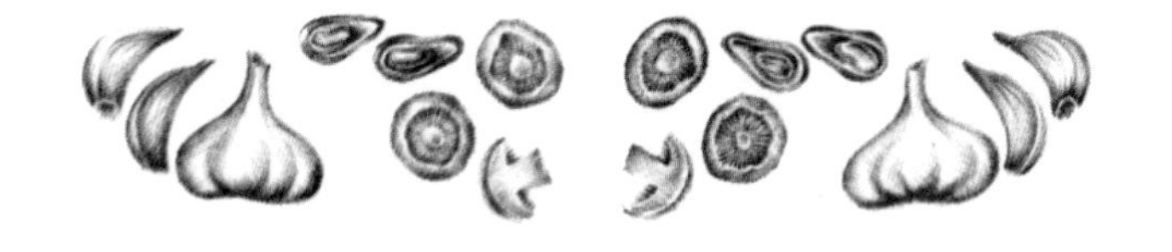

• NECTARINES •

These are a smooth-skinned variety of peach similar in colouring but with a fuller flavour.

See also PEACHES.

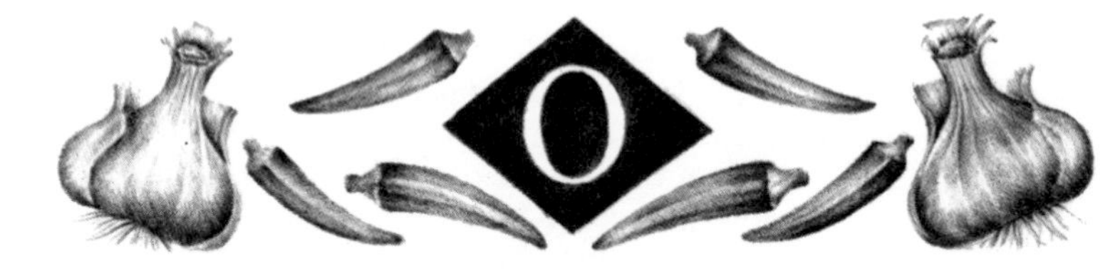

• OFFAL •

See KIDNEYS, LIVER etc.

• OKRA •

Okra, also known as Lady's fingers, are five-sided green tapering pods. Choose firm, bright pods avoiding any which are soft or with brown marks as this is a sign of staleness. Wash and dry them well, then trim off the stalk (stem) end. If you want to cook them whole, then take care not to cut into the pod as you prepare the okra or the gluey sap will ooze out during cooking and the vegetables are likely to lose their shape. If you intend adding them to stews this does not matter as the sap will help to thicken the sauce.

Most frequently used in stews or cooked with tomatoes, okra is also excellent when cooked and served like asparagus with a Hollandaise Sauce. But the okra must be young and absolutely fresh or they may be stringy.

TO COOK Rinse 225 g/8 oz okra but do not trim off the stalk (stem). Put into a dish with 3 tablespoons water, cover with cling film (plastic wrap), leaving a small gap for the steam to escape, and cook on full power for 4–5 minutes until tender but firm, stirring once. Drain. Using the stalk (stem) as a handle, dip each one into Hollandaise Sauce (see page 179) and eat all but the conical cap and stalk (stem) which should be discarded.

• OMELETTES •

An omelette cooked in the microwave has a creamier though closer, firmer texture than one cooked in a omelette pan. It lacks the golden brown flecked base of a conventionally cooked one.

TO COOK Put 1 tablespoon butter into an 18–20-cm/7–8-in shallow glass dish and heat for 30 seconds to melt. Beat 3 eggs to blend and season with salt and pepper. Turn into the dish and cook on full power for 1 minute. Lift and stir to bring the uncooked centre to the outer edge. Cook for another minute or until set to your taste. You may well feel that you have more control over the stirring, tilting and cooking of an omelette if it is in a pan rather than in the microwave.

• ONIONS •

Choose firm onions with dry papery skins, rejecting any that are softening or sprouting. English or American onions have a strong flavour; those from Spain and other warmer climates such as Bermuda are mild. The microwave softens them quickly and contains the smell. When adding to dishes, use chopped onion rather than sliced; this blends better with other ingredients.

The easiest way to chop an onion is to cut a thin slice from the top and peel off (remove) the skin. Halve the onion and place the halves cut side down on a board. Without cutting through the root, cut several slices from top to bottom and vertical to the board. Then slice across horizontally two or three times. Finally cut across at right angles so the onion falls into small dice.

TO SOFTEN A CHOPPED ONION Put a medium onion, cut as above, in a dish with 1 tablespoon oil and cook on full power for 2–3 minutes. Use as required.

• BOILED ONIONS •

Take a slice off the top of 4 medium onions (about 175 g/6 oz each), peel (skin) and remove the root ends. Place the onions in a dish with 2 tablespoons water. Cover with cling film (plastic wrap), leaving a small gap for the steam to escape, and cook on full power for 7–8 minutes until the onions are tender but still firm. Drain and serve.

• GLAZED ONIONS •

Peel (skin) 225 g/8 oz tiny pickling (small white) onions. A tearsome process! Try pouring boiling water over them, leaving for 5 minutes, then draining, when the skins should slip off easily. Arrange in a dish in a single layer. Dot with 25 g/1 oz/2 tablespoons butter and sprinkle 2 teaspoons sugar over them. Cover with cling film (plastic wrap), leaving a small gap for the steam to escape, and cook on full power for 3 minutes. Stir, leave uncovered and cook for a further 3–5 minutes until tender and glistening. Leaving the onions uncovered for the final cooking allows some of the moisture to evaporate so that the buttery juices are not too diluted.

• STUFFED ONIONS •

Cut a slice off the top of 4 medium onions (about 175 g/6 oz each). Peel (skin) and trim off the root ends. Put in a dish with 2 tablespoons water, cover with cling film (plastic wrap), leaving a small gap for the steam to escape, and cook on full power for 7–8 minutes until softened. Remove and cool the very hot onions under running cold water to make them easier to handle. Turn upside down and drain. Rinse out the dish.

Halve and core 4 small lambs' kidneys and remove the membrane. You will only need two if they are large. Snip 2 slices of rindless streaky bacon into small pieces.

Turn the onions over and, with a teaspoon, scoop out the centres leaving just two or three outer layers intact. Take care – they are rather fragile now they are softened. Push a kidney into the centre of each and top with bacon pieces. Arrange the onions in the dish, cover with cling film (plastic wrap), leaving a small gap for the steam to escape, and cook on full power for 3–4 minutes. Stand for 2 minutes.

Provide a pot of prepared mustard, salt and pepper and let each person season their onion as they eat it.

• OXTAIL •

This needs long slow cooking in liquid to tenderise it and should be done conventionally.

• PANCAKES •

Pancakes need a hot surface to set and brown them so cook them conventionally. Use the microwave for preparing fillings and reheating prepared pancakes.

• PARSNIPS •

Parsnips should be firm and unblemished and of medium size. Wash them, trim off the top and bottom and peel (pare) them. If they are to be puréed, cut them into cubes. If they are to be served buttered or roasted, halve – or quarter if very large – and remove the centre if it is woody.

• CREAMED PARSNIPS •

Place 450 g/1 lb cubed parsnips in a dish with 4 tablespoons water. Cover with cling film (plastic wrap), leaving a small gap for the steam to escape, and cook on full power for 7–9 minutes, stirring once or twice. Stand for 3 minutes, drain and mash with a little butter. Season with salt and pepper and serve.

• BUTTERED PARSNIPS •

Arrange 450 g/1 lb halved or quartered parsnips in a dish with the thinner ends towards the centre. Add 3 tablespoons water, cover with cling film (plastic wrap), leaving a small gap for the steam to escape, and cook on full power for 8–10 minutes. Drain. Add 40 g/1½ oz/3 tablespoons butter to the parsnips, turning them until it melts and coats them. Season and serve.

• ROAST PARSNIPS •

Arrange 450 g/1 lb halved or quartered parnsips in a dish with the thinner ends towards the centre. Add 3 tablespoons water, cover and cook on full power for 3 minutes. Drain and transfer to a roasting tin (pan) containing hot dripping. Turn the parsnips over in the fat to coat them and cook in a moderately hot oven (190 C, 375 F, gas 5) for about 30–40 minutes.

• PARTRIDGE •

This small game bird should only be roasted when young. It weighs up to about 400 g/14 oz. You will need one per person. Put 1 tablespoon butter in the body cavity, truss it and tie a strip of pork fat or streaky (fat) bacon over the breast. Follow the cooking instructions for pheasant (see page 97).

• PASTA •

It's no quicker to cook pasta in the microwave but it is a clean and convenient method because the pasta will not stick and is unlikely to boil over.

Pasta needs to be cooked in plenty of boiling water so you will need a large (at least 3-litre/5-pint/6-pint capacity) ovenproof bowl. Boil the water in an electric kettle – it's quicker than by microwave. Check half-way through the cooking to see that all the pasta is under the water. As with most microwave cooking, the standing time is important because it completes the cooking.

TO COOK Place 225 g/8 oz dry pasta in a large ovenproof bowl and pour over it 1.75 litres/3 pints/3½ pints boiling water. Long strands of spaghetti or vermicelli must be pushed down into the water as the lower part softens. Stir in 1 teaspoon salt and 1 tablespoon oil. Cover with cling film (plastic wrap), leaving a small gap for the steam to escape, and cook on full power for the recommended times. Drain after standing, return it to the hot bowl and toss in a little oil or butter until it glistens. Season well and serve.

Lasagne should be cooked in an oblong or square dish and only needs 1.15 litres/2 pints/2½ pints boiling water. Add 1 teaspoon salt and 1 tablespoon oil as with the other pastas. Drain well and use as required. Alternatively use the 'no pre-cooking' lasagne and simply layer it with a sauce before cooking.

Tagliatelle and Vermicelli	5 minutes on full power, 5 minutes standing
Spaghetti, Fusili and short pasta shapes	9 minutes on full power, 8 minutes standing
Lasagne: 9 sheets	5 minutes on full power, 5 minutes standing.

• PASTRY •

Pastry is much better in taste, texture and colour when cooked conventionally.

Shortcrust pastry (basic pie dough) is not only pallid but in most cases lacks the flavour and short crispness that dry heat gives it. Puff pastry, too, is unappetisingly pale and though crisp lacks flavour. The browning process which occurs in conventional baking contributes not only colour but flavour.

Suet pastry works well in the microwave for recipes requiring moist heat like a roly-poly or a suet pudding. But you can't use suet crust for a 'baked' pie in the microwave.

• PEACHES •

Choose peaches that are firm rather than soft. They should have smooth, velvety skins that are yellow to orange with a faint blush. If not quite ripe, their flavour will be improved if poached gently in a light sugar syrup before being used.

TO POACH Put 75 g/3 oz/$\frac{1}{3}$ cup sugar in a deep dish, pour in 600 ml/1 pint/1$\frac{1}{4}$ pints boiling water and stir to dissolve. Add a vanilla pod and cook on full power for 2–3 minutes. Put 4 peaches in a bowl and pour boiling water over them. Leave for 30 seconds or so, drain and cool under running cold water and the skins should slip off.

Halve, stone (seed) and drop the peaches into the syrup. Remove the vanilla pod. Cover the dish with cling film (plastic wrap), leaving a small gap for the steam to escape, and cook on full power for 2–3 minutes depending on the ripeness of the fruit. Leave to cool in the syrup and use as required.

Drained and served with a purée of raspberries and vanilla ice cream will turn them into Peach Melba.

• PEARS •

These are best lightly poached in a sugar syrup. Most pears have a delicate flavour and are improved if cooked in cider or wine and sugar rather than in water.

Peel, halve and core the pears and leave in acidulated water (600 ml/1 pint/1$\frac{1}{4}$ pints water to 2 tablespoons lemon juice) until ready to cook so they do not discolour.

To cook Pour 300 ml/½ pint/1¼ cups cider or red wine into a dish, add 100 g/4 oz/½ cup sugar, cover with cling-film (plastic wrap), leaving a small gap for the steam to escape, and cook on full power for 5–6 minutes, stirring once. Arrange the prepared pears in the syrup, narrow ends towards the centre, cover with cling film (plastic wrap), leaving a small gap for the steam to escape, and cook on full power for 8–10 minutes, rearranging the pears and turning them over half-way through the cooking. Timing will depend on the ripeness of the pears. Cool.

• PEAS (GREEN) •

Choose well-filled, bright pods and shell (hull) them just prior to cooking. You will need 450–675 g/1–1½ lb to yield 225 g/8 oz/1 cup prepared peas.

To cook Put in a dish with 25 g/1 oz/2 tablespoons butter or water. Cover with cling film (plastic wrap), leaving a small gap for steam to escape. Cook on full power 4–5 minutes. Stand for 2 minutes. Season and serve.

See also MANGE-TOUT (SNOW) PEAS.

• PEPPERS (SWEET BELL) •

Choose peppers with firm, glossy skins rejecting any dull wrinkled ones. The colour denotes the degree of ripeness, the red being the ripest and sweetest.

They are particularly good when filled with a savoury stuffing.

Stuffed Peppers

Slice the tops off 4 small peppers and remove the seeds and white pith (membrane). Rinse out and put in a dish with 4 tablespoons water, cover with cling film (plastic wrap), leaving a small gap for steam to escape. Cook on full power for 3–4 minutes to just soften. Drain, leaving about 2 tablespoons water in the dish.

Put 1 tablespoon oil in a dish with a finely chopped small onion and cook on full power for 2 minutes. Add 50 g/2 oz/½ cup chopped mushrooms and cook for 1 minute. Stir in 75 g/3 oz/1½ cups cooked brown rice and 25 g/1 oz/¼ cup chopped toasted almonds. Season with salt and pepper and a little soy sauce and pile the mixture into the peppers. Cover with cling film (plastic wrap), leaving a small gap for the steam to escape, and cook on full power for 5 minutes. Stand for 2 minutes and serve.

• PHEASANT •

Make sure you get a young bird for roasting; older ones are likely to be tough and are best conventionally casseroled. If you buy them ready-prepared, they will have been hung to give them their gamey flavour, essential if the bird is to be roasted or it will be insipid. They are usually sold as a brace but can be bought singly. The hen is plumper and more tender than the cock and is generally considered to have a better flavour, so a hen is the one to choose for roasting. All game is dry and even a young bird will need a covering of fat. It will take 6–7 minutes per 450 g/1 lb to cook.

A ready-prepared pheasant will be trussed and should have fat tied over its breast; if not, cover with slices of streaky (fat) bacon.

TO COOK Put 1 tablespoon butter in the body cavity of a 900-g/2-lb pheasant. Put breast side down in a dish that can be transferred to the conventional oven later. Cover with greaseproof (waxed) paper and cook on full power for 7 minutes. Turn it over and cook for a further 6 minutes. Remove the paper and bacon and baste again, then put in a hot oven (220 C, 425 F, gas 7) for 10 minutes to brown and crisp the skin.

To make the gravy, pour off the fat, leaving the sediment behind, blend in a dusting of flour and then gradually stir in 300 ml/$\frac{1}{2}$ pint/$1\frac{1}{4}$ cups stock. Cook on full power for 3–4 minutes, stirring once. Check seasoning before serving.

• PIGEON •

Pigeon is available all the year round and, provided it is young, it can be cooked in the microwave in the same way as game birds. Like them, its flesh is dry and needs a covering of pork fat or bacon before cooking. Cook it in the same way as PHEASANT above.

• PILCHARDS •

See SARDINES.

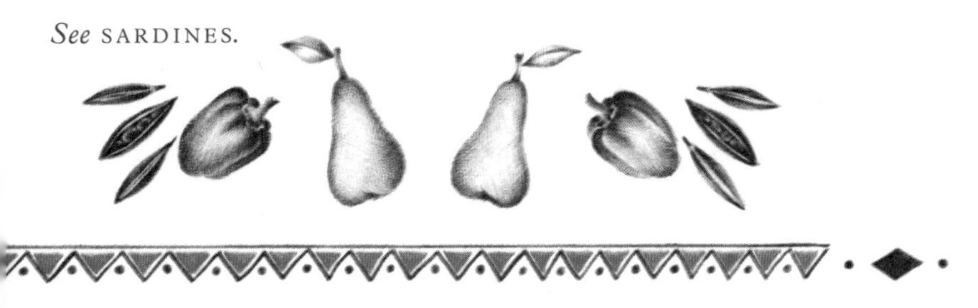

• PIZZA •

Pizzas can be cooked in the microwave but the dough bases will be soft. This can be partially overcome by cooking them in a browning dish or a griddle, though the top edges will not have the conventional crusty finish. They do, however, cook extremely quickly and with a well-flavoured topping can make a tasty snack meal.

To make two (18-cm/7-in) pizzas you will need 450 g/1 lb of risen bread dough. Divide it in two and roll out to two 18-cm/7-in circles. Set aside while you make the topping. Grate 50 g/2 oz/½ cup Cheddar cheese or thinly slice 50 g/2 oz/½ cup Mozzarella. Open a can of anchovy fillets. Turn 1 (397-g/14-oz) can/2 cups canned tomatoes into a sieve to drain off all the juices and break up the tomatoes with a spoon. Put 1 finely chopped medium onion into a dish with 1 tablespoon oil. Cover with cling film (plastic wrap), leaving a small gap for the steam to escape, and cook on full power for 3 minutes until softened. Stir the tomatoes into the onions together with 2 tablespoons basil-flavoured tomato purée and season with salt and pepper. Cook for 3–4 minutes on full power, stirring once. It should be fairly dry.

Heat the browning dish or pizza browner according to the manufacturers' instructions and press one of the dough rounds on to the base. Cook on full power for 1 minute. Turn it over and spread half the tomato mixture over it to within 2.5 cm/1 in of the edge. Sprinkle half the cheese over, then arrange a lattice of anchovy fillets on the top. Cook on full power for 2 minutes. Repeat with the second pizza base.

If your browning dish was not sufficiently hot to brown the second side of the dough, reheat the dish, put in the pizza and cook on full power for 1 minute.By doing this you achieve a pleasantly crisp base.

• PLAICE OR FLOUNDER •

A popular small flat fish which is sold whole or filleted. If cooked whole the dark skin should be removed (see how to do this under SOLE on page 112). It has a mild flavour so, if plainly cooked, serve with wedges of lemon to squeeze over it.

TO COOK Arrange 450 g/1 lb of whole plaice on a plate or dish with the tails to the centre and overlapping if necessary. Cover with cling film (plastic wrap), leaving a small gap for the steam to escape, and cook on full power for 3–4 minutes. Leave to stand for 2 minutes. The fish is cooked if the flesh is firm and opaque. If it is transparent, cook a little longer.

• POUSSIN •

This is the French name for a 4–6 week-old chicken weighing about 450 g/1 lb. Cook in the same way as chicken, see page 59.

• PLUMS •

See GREENGAGES.

• PORK •

A large piece of pork can be cooked in the microwave but even oiling and salting the rind will not produce the crisp crackling of a conventional roast. So cook your meat in the microwave for speed, then finish it in a hot oven for crisp golden crackling.

If possible choose a cut that is the same thickness throughout as it will cook more evenly. If this is not possible, shield the thinner areas with small pieces of foil once they are cooked so they don't dry out.

You need to lift the meat off the base of the dish so that it does not cook in its own juices. Do this in one of the following ways:

☐ stand it on a roasting rack over a shallow dish and cover it with a slit roasting bag tented over it.

☐ stand the meat on one or, if necessary, two upturned plain saucers and cover with a slit roasting bag or greaseproof (waxed) paper.

TIMING about 9–10 minutes per 450 g/1 lb.

Pork must always be well cooked. A standing time of about 20 minutes will complete the cooking. For greater accuracy use a microwave thermometer which is sold with a chart giving two temperatures. The first is the temperature the meat should have reached at the end of the cooking time and the second the temperature it should reach after standing.

TO COOK A ROAST Rub the skin with a little oil and salt and stand the meat on a roasting rack over a dish. Cover with a slit roasting bag or piece of greaseproof (waxed) paper and cook on full power for 12 minutes. Turn the meat round, drain off any fat and juices and cook for another 15 minutes. Remove covering and transfer the meat to a roasting tin (pan). Cook in a moderately hot oven (200C, 400F, gas 6) for about 30 minutes when the crackling should be crisp and golden and the roast fully cooked.

An apple sauce can be made in the microwave while the meat finishes cooking. A quick recipe using whole apples is under DUCK on page 67, another using sliced apples on page 40.

• PORK CHOPS •

These will be moist and tender cooked in the microwave though rather grey in appearance. Use a browning dish or grill (broiler) to colour them.

• TENDERLOIN •

Also known as pork fillet, this is a tender cut and can be cooked whole, cut into chunks or flattened out in escalopes. Again the colour will be unappetising so use a browning dish or frying pan (skillet) for preliminary browning unless the meat is cooked in a sauce.

See also MEAT.

• POTATOES •

Potatoes can be 'baked' and boiled in the microwave but they cannot be fried or roasted.

• JACKET POTATOES •

These are probably the most popular because in small numbers they can be cooked in a fraction of the time it takes conventionally. The skins will not be crisp but the flavour of the potato is very good.

Wash and dry the potatoes and prick them or the skins will burst. Stand on absorbent kitchen paper on the floor of the cooker and, if cooking several, arrange evenly spaced in a circle. Here are the cooking times for a potato weighing 150 g/5 oz cooked on full power.

1 potato will take 5 minutes • 2 potatoes will take 6–8 minutes
3 potatoes will take 9–10 minutes.
4 potatoes will take 10–11 minutes

The cooking times for a potato weighing 350 g/12 oz are as follows:

1 potato will take 8 minutes • 2 potatoes will take 15 minutes
3 potatoes will take 21 minutes.
4 potatoes will take 27 minutes.

If cooking 4 potatoes, rearrange them once or twice during cooking. There is no need to turn smaller quantities.

• BOILED POTATOES •

Wash, peel (pare) and cut 450 g/1 lb potatoes into even-sized pieces. Put them in a dish with 4 tablespoons water. Cover with cling film (plastic wrap), leaving a small gap for the steam to escape, and cook on full power for 8–10 minutes, stirring once. Drain, season and serve.

• CREAMED POTATOES •

Wash, peel (pare) and cut 450 g/1 lb potatoes into small cubes. Put into a dish with 3 tablespoons water. Cover with cling film (plastic wrap), leaving a small gap for the steam to escape, and cook on full power for 8–10 minutes, stirring once. Stand for 2 minutes, drain and mash with 15 g/½ oz/1 tablespoon butter, a little milk, salt and pepper.

• NEW POTATOES •

Wash 450 g/1 lb potatoes and prick the skins. Place in a dish with 2 tablespoons water and a small sprig of mint. Cover with cling film (plastic wrap), leaving a small gap for the steam to escape, and cook on full power for 7–9 minutes. Drain, season and serve with butter. Don't overcook new potatoes or they will be spongy.

• CHIPS (FRENCH FRIES) •

A small quantity at a time can be cooked in a browning dish but they will not be as crisp as when conventionally fried. Deep frying must never be attempted in the microwave. There is no control over the temperature, so for really crisp chips cook them conventionally.

• POULTRY •

All poultry can be cooked in the microwave provided it is young and tender. Older birds should be casseroled or boiled conventionally.

The flesh of the bird keeps beautifully moist and has a good taste and texture but the absence of dry heat means the skin will not brown and crisp. Overcome this by cooking the bird first in the microwave and transferring it to a hot oven to finish the cooking and brown and crisp the skin.

If the bird is stuffed, add an extra minute or two to the cooking time. All poultry must be trussed to keep it in shape during cooking and this can be done by using either string or wooden – never metal – skewers.

Turn the bird at least once during cooking, two or three times for a turkey, to ensure even cooking and check that no parts are overcooking. Wing tips are particularly vulnerable and these may need covering with small pieces of foil so they do not dry out. It is important to make sure that the foil cannot touch the sides of the cooker.

Fatty birds like duck and geese need pricking so the fat can drain away. All birds should be raised on a rack or upturned saucers so they do not sit in their own juices. Drain the juices off periodically as they attract microwave energy and slow down the cooking.

It is not absolutely necessary to cover poultry but, as there is always a certain amount of spattering, a covering of some sort will contain it and keep the oven clean.

All poultry can be cooked on full power but if you have a cooker with variable power, a different setting may be indicated. Always be guided by the manufacturers' recommendations on this point.

Suggested timings are given under the individual entries. For greater accuracy use a meat thermometer. If it is to be used inside the cooker, it must be the special microwave thermometer, never an ordinary meat thermometer.

Standing time is important because the temperature continues to rise at this stage and the cooking continues. If the bird is transferred to a hot oven for browning and crisping that time counts as the standing time.

Make sure frozen poultry is completely thawed before cooking.

See also CHICKEN, DUCK, GOOSE and TURKEY.

• PRAWNS (SHRIMPS) •

These are usually sold ready-cooked but they can be reheated briefly quite successfully. Don't overcook or they will toughen. Here is one way to serve them that is both quick to prepare and cook.

Prawns in Garlic Butter

Divide 225 g/8 oz peeled cooked prawns between four ramekin dishes (custard cups). Blend together 50 g/2 oz/$\frac{1}{4}$ cup butter and a crushed garlic clove in a small bowl. Heat on full power for 1–2 minutes until melted. Stir in 2 tablespoons chopped parsley and pour or spoon over the prawns. Heat the buttery prawns on full power for 2 minutes and serve with plenty of crusty French bread to mop up the juices.

Note If using frozen prawns, thaw them first, drain and pat dry on absorbent kitchen paper before using. If thawed and heated at the same time, they will make the buttery juice too watery.

• PRESERVES •

See CHUTNEY, JAM and MARMALADE.

• PUDDINGS (DESSERTS) •

Not only can the microwave be used to cook a wide range of puddings but it can speed up the preparation of many others by thawing fruit, softening gelatine and melting chocolate.

Traditional puddings like the steamed suet variety will be well risen and light and cooked in minutes rather than hours. A sponge that takes only 5 minutes to cook can be transformed with cream, fruits and liqueur into a party pudding.

Fruits which are to be served on their own with yogurt or cream cook extremely well and are rich in colour and flavour. You may have reservations over fruits like gooseberries and plums, as their skins do not soften so well in the microwave.

Pastry is not successful so bake your fruit pies in the conventional cooker. Fruit crumbles can be microwaved for speed if you do nòt mind a soft topping or are prepared to grill (broil) it for a minute or two after cooking.

Slightly trickier are egg custards but with careful timing and gentle cooking, they can be meltingly soft and delicious.

Rice pudding fans should try the version on page 107. It has an incomparable rich creaminess.

More pudding ideas in the recipe section (see pages 167–76).

• PULSES (DRIED BEANS) •

Pulses, with the exception of lentils, need soaking before cooking and, although this usually takes several hours, it can be speeded up in the microwave. Put the pulses in a bowl, cover with cold water, bring to the boil, stand for 1 hour, drain. Cover with fresh water and cook. Timings can vary considerably from 40 minutes to over 1 hour, depending on the age of the beans. Results are variable with the skins tending to be tough.

• QUAIL •

Quail are tiny birds weighing about 100 g/4 oz each, so you will need two per person, unless boned and stuffed when one would suffice. Most of the quail bought today are farmed. They are plump and tender and available all the year round.

TO PREPARE Wash and pat them dry. Skewer the legs to the body with wooden cocktail sticks (toothpicks). Smear the breasts with butter or cover with streaky (fat) bacon.

TO COOK Place 4 quail in a dish, cover with cling film (plastic wrap), leaving a small gap for the steam to escape, and cook on full power for 6–8 minutes, rearranging once during cooking. During their standing time they can be lightly coloured under the grill (broiler) or, if it is already on, in the oven. Serve each one on a round of toast or fried bread (toasted croûton) with thin gravy.

• RABBIT •

Most of the rabbit now available is tame and consequently tender. It can be casseroled in the same way as chicken and with its rather bland flavour, benefits from being cooked in full-bodied sauces. Rabbit can replace chicken in the recipe on page 60 or can be cooked in a mustard sauce.

It reheats very well and if anything tastes even creamier.

RABBIT IN MUSTARD SAUCE

Put 1 tablespoon oil and 1 finely chopped small onion in a dish, cover with cling film (plastic wrap), leaving a small gap for the steam to escape, and cook on full power for 3 minutes. Stir in 1 tablespoon flour and 1 tablespoon French (Dijon) mustard. Blend in 150 ml/$\frac{1}{4}$ pint/$\frac{2}{3}$ cup white wine or chicken stock and season with salt and pepper. Add 4 rabbit joints to the sauce fleshy side downwards. Cover with cling film (plastic wrap), leaving a small gap for the steam to escape, and cook on full power for 25 minutes. Stir and re-position twice during the cooking.

• REDCURRANTS •

These are often combined with raspberries in pies, puddings and ices but are good on their own when fully ripe. Cook in the same way as blackcurrants (see page 50).

• RED KIDNEY BEANS •

See PULSES.

• RHUBARB •

The long stalks of vividly pink, forced rhubarb arrive in the shops in late winter and early spring. It can be quickly cooked in the microwave though the colour seems to intensify to an even more lurid pink. The first garden rhubarb arriving a little later is pink, too, but a much more restrained shade. Later the stalks thicken and coarsen and the colour is much darker. At this stage it tends to be tough and stringy.

When cooked in the microwave, rhubarb needs no water other than what clings to it after washing, so it retains all its flavour and plenty of colour.

Cut off the leaves, which are inedible, and trim the base of any brownish bits. Cut the rhubarb into pieces removing any strings at the same time.

TO COOK Put 450g/1lb prepared rhubarb in a dish with 100g/4oz/½ cup sugar and cover with cling film (plastic wrap), leaving a small gap for the steam to escape. Cook on full power for 4–6 minutes until tender but still holding its shape. Timing will depend on the age and thickness of the sticks (stalks). Stand for 2 minutes.

• RICE •

Very little time is saved by cooking rice in the microwave but it doesn't need stirring, won't stick and, provided you use a large enough bowl, it won't boil over. In the microwave rice is cooked by the absorption method. This means that instead of being boiled in a large quantity of water, which is drained off once the rice is cooked, the rice is just covered with water and cooked until it has all been absorbed. Stock can be used instead of water.

TO COOK 225 G/8 OZ LONG-GRAIN RICE Put the rice into a large ovenproof bowl. Bring 600ml/1 pint/1¼ pints water to the boil (quickest in an electric kettle), pour it over the rice, add 1 teaspoon salt and stir. Cover with cling film (plastic wrap), leaving a small gap for the steam to escape, and cook on full power for 10 minutes. Stand, covered, for 10 minutes. Use a fork to fluff up the grains of rice which should have absorbed all the water.

TO COOK 225 G / 8 OZ BASMATI RICE Wash and drain the rice thoroughly, then follow the instructions for long-grain rice, cooking for the same time.

TO COOK 225 G / 8 OZ BROWN RICE Use 750 ml/ 1¼ pints/ 1½ pints boiling water with 1 teaspoon salt and cook as for long-grain rice, allowing 25 minutes on full power with a standing time of 10 minutes.

• RICE PUDDING •

This is totally successful and trouble free when cooked in the microwave. Just make sure you use a large enough bowl because in the initial cooking on full power the milk rises and could bubble over.

TO COOK Measure 50 g/2 oz/¼ cup pudding rice into a large ovenproof glass bowl. Stir in 25 g/1 oz/1 tablespoon sugar and 600 ml/1 pint/2½ cups milk. Cover with cling film (plastic wrap), leaving a small gap for the steam to escape, and cook on full power for 8–10 minutes until it is boiling. Stir well, re-cover and cook on low power (30%) for 30–35 minutes, stirring every 10 minutes. Stand for 5 minutes.

Skin lovers may feel deprived but not for long when they discover how soft, creamy and unbelievably delicious rice pudding cooked this way can be.

• ROES •

Soft roes, such as herring or flounder, make a tasty and nutritious snack and will cook in the microwave while the bread is being toasted.

Wash the roes carefully, pulling away any threads. Dry on absorbent kitchen paper.

TO COOK Put 15 g/$\frac{1}{2}$ oz/1 tablespoon butter in a dish and heat on full power until melted, about 30 seconds. Add 225 g/8 oz prepared roes and turn over in the butter. Cover with cling film (plastic wrap), leaving a small gap for the steam to escape, and cook on full power for 2 minutes, stirring once. Stand for 1 minute, then pile on to hot toast. Season with salt, pepper and a squeeze of lemon juice.

• SALMON •

Wild salmon and salmon trout are seasonal fish but farmed salmon is available throughout the year. Its oily, bright pink to red flesh is best when simply cooked. Serve it hot with butter or Hollandaise sauce or cold with mayonnaise.

Sea trout, often labelled salmon trout because of its similarity in looks and colour, has possibly a finer flavour than salmon, though it costs slightly less.

You need a large capacity oven without a turntable to cook a whole salmon; otherwise the salmon must be curved into a dish for cooking – it will, of course, remain curved once cooked. The alternative – if you want to present the whole salmon cold – is to cut it in two, cook the two pieces either in a roasting bag or on a large plate and when they are cold, skin and fillet them and arrange on a dish, putting the two pieces together again. If you just tease the flesh very gently with a knife point over the cut, you can successfully hide it and any garnish can complete the disguise. Cover the whole fish with wafer-thin slices of peeled cucumber to simulate the fish scales. Mayonnaise, cucumber or prawns (shrimps) can also be used to good effect.

All you will need to do with a prepared salmon is rinse it well.

TO COOK A WHOLE SALMON Put a 1.25-kg/2½-lb salmon, cut if necessary, on to a large plate or dish. Add 2–3 tablespoons water, cover with cling film (plastic wrap), leaving a small gap for the steam to escape, and cook on full power for 10 minutes, rearranging the pieces or turning the whole fish half-way through the cooking. Put a small piece of foil around the tail if necessary. Leave until cold, then skin, fillet and garnish.

TO COOK SALMON STEAKS Put 40 g/1½ oz/3 tablespoons butter in a dish and heat on full power for 1 minute until melted. Put two (175-g/6-oz) steaks in the dish, narrow ends to the centre. Turn them over in the melted butter. Cover with cling film (plastic wrap), leaving a small gap for the steam to escape, and cook on full power for 3 minutes, turning once. Stand for 1 minute. Season and serve with the buttery juices poured over them.

• SARDINES •

These are small, round oily fish which when mature are called pilchards. They are really best when crisply grilled (broiled) but can be cooked in the microwave if you do not mind the soft skin. Slash the skin once or twice on each side and cook on full power allowing about 4 minutes per 450 g/1 lb.

• SAUCES •

Sauces are far less demanding when cooked in the microwave. They are quick, there is no need for constant stirring, no risk of their sticking and little chance of their lumping. In fact the microwave is put to really effective use in sauce-making.

When using cornflour (cornstarch), flour or arrowroot as a base, always make sure they are blended smoothly and completely with the liquid before heating them. You will then only need to stir or whisk (beat) a couple of times during cooking to ensure a lump-free sauce.

See Sauces chapter on page 177–83.

• SAUSAGES •

These cook quickly in the microwave but don't look very appetising. Use a browning dish to improve the colour and give some crispness, though you will not get the dark brown crispness of a conventionally fried sausage.

Prick them before cooking or the skins will burst and wrinkle back off the meat.

TO COOK Heat a browning dish for 3 minutes or as recommended by the manufacturer. Put in 4 large sausages, pressing them down on to the dish and then turning them to brown all over, cover and cook for 2 minutes. Turn and cook for another 2 minutes. Serve.

• SCALLOPS •

Fresh scallops are usually sold opened, displayed on their half shell. The flesh should be moist and white, the coral a pinky orange.

As the coral needs only a very short cooking time, remove it and add to the dish for the last minute. Slice the white through into two discs or, if very large, cut into quarters.

TO COOK Put the white flesh only of 225 g/8 oz scallops in a dish, cover with cling film (plastic wrap), leaving a small gap for the steam to escape, and cook for 1½ minutes. Stir the scallops and add the coral, cover and cook for a further 1 minute. Leave to stand while you make a sauce.

Put 15 g/½ oz/1 tablespoon butter in a bowl and heat on full power for 30 seconds until melted. Stir in 1 tablespoon flour, blend in the cooking liquid from the scallops and 2 tablespoons dry white wine. Cook on full power for 2 minutes, stirring once, season and stir in 2 tablespoons cream and cook for a further 1 minute. Pour over the scallops and serve.

• SCONES (HOT BISCUITS) •

Although these rise well and are quite light, they don't have the firm, crisp and coloured surface of a conventionally baked scone. If you want to try them, they look and taste better made with either all wholemeal or a fifty-fifty mixture of wholemeal and white flour. A batch of eight scones will take about 4 minutes to cook on full power. Expect the base of the scones to be moist after cooking. They should dry out as they stand. Should be eaten while still warm, they toughen on cooling.

• SHELLFISH •

See FISH AND SHELLFISH.

• SHORTBREAD (SHORTCAKE) •

This is not a total success in the microwave. If you cook it long enough to make it crisp, it will be brown through the centre. If it is cooked to an even paleness all through, it will be soft and lack the buttery taste and texture of a true shortbread.

Cooking on low power (30%) gave a more even cooking result, though the base was rather greasy and soft. Further cooking didn't remedy this it simply overcooked the rest.

• SHRIMPS •

These tiny but delicious shellfish are usually sold cooked by the fishmonger. If you have the patience to prepare a large quantity turn them into potted shrimps for four this way.

Potted Shrimps

In a large ovenproof bowl place 115 g/4½ oz/½–⅔ cup butter. Cook on full power for 2 minutes. Mix in 1.15 litres/2 pints/5 cups peeled cooked shrimps, 1 teaspoon ground mace, ¼ teaspoon cayenne and salt to taste – about ¼ to ½ teaspoon. Cover with cling film (plastic wrap), leaving a small gap for the steam to escape, and cook for 1 minute. Stir well and cook for another minute. Divide the mixture evenly between four small ramekin dishes (custard cups).

Cook 40 g/1½ oz/3 tablespoons butter in a small glass bowl for 1 minute. Strain through a single layer of absorbent kitchen paper, then pour on top of the potted shrimps to seal. Chill for 1 to 2 days before serving.

You can treat prawns in the same way.

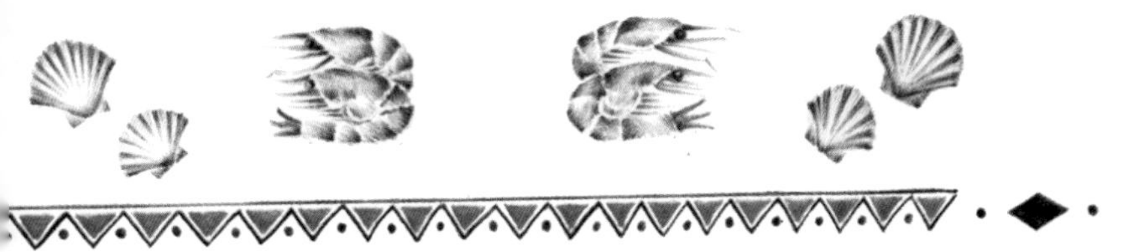

• SNOW PEAS •

See MANGE-TOUT PEAS.

• SOLE •

This is considered the best of all the flat white fish with its firm flesh and delicate flavour. The skin is a greyish brown. Lemon sole is smaller and more rounded in shape with a lighter brown skin. It too has a firm white flesh though the flavour is not quite so delicate.

Sole can be cooked whole or in fillets which can be stuffed and rolled. Like all white fish it cooks quickly and perfectly in the microwave.

The dark skin should be removed before cooking. To do this, cut through the skin at the tail, then work your finger round the edge to loosen the skin. Hold the fleshy side with one hand. Dip the fingers of your other hand in salt to prevent them slipping, grip the skin and pull it back and off the flesh. Rinse the fish.

TO COOK Place a 350 g/12 oz sole on a plate or dish, dot with butter, cover with cling film (plastic wrap), leaving a small gap for the steam to escape, and cook on full power for 3 minutes. Stand for 1 minute, then check if the flesh is cooked. It should be white and firm. If it is transparent, cook a little longer. Season and serve with a slice of lemon.

• SOUFFLÉS •

These cannot be cooked in the microwave but you can use it to make the base sauce of butter, flour and milk.

• SOUPS •

Most soups can be made in the microwave with the exception of those using the tougher cuts of meat. These need long, slow conventional cooking to release their flavours and soften them.

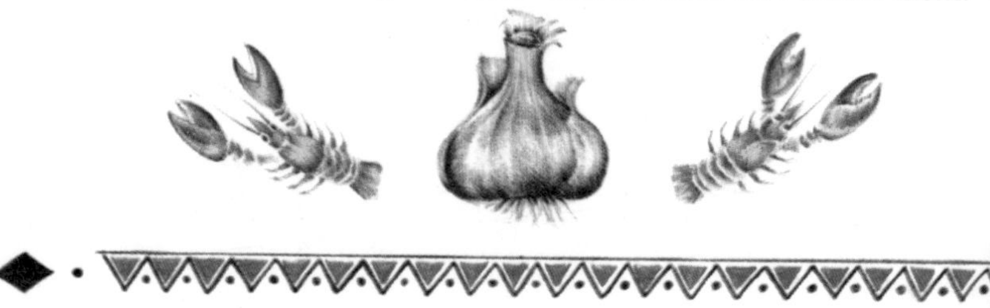

Don't heat quantities of liquid in the microwave: it takes too long. Use hot stock or water that has been heated in a saucepan or kettle.

When adapting recipes to microwaving, you will probably need to cut down on the liquid because with the quicker cooking there is less evaporation. When adding the liquid to the ingredients, keep some back until the soup has almost finished cooking, then add just sufficient to give the right flavour and consistency. Do the same with cream soups. Cook the ingredients in a small quantity of liquid, blend to a purée and thin as necessary.

A good stock is the best base for home-made soups and these can be quickly made in the microwave.

See STOCKS.

• SPINACH •

Make sure the leaves are fresh, green and crisp, discarding any wilted ones. Pull away the midrib and wash the leaves in several changes of water to remove sand or grit. Shake off excess water. The water on the leaves will be sufficient for cooking.

TO COOK Put 450g/1lb prepared spinach in a boiling or roasting bag and loosely secure the end with an elastic band. Stand the bag in the microwave and cook on full power for 5–7 minutes, giving it a shake half-way through the cooking. Tip the spinach into a colander to drain, pressing it well to extract the moisture. Season, add a knob of butter and serve.

• SPRING GREENS •

These are young cabbages sold before the hearts have developed. They must be crisp and fresh. If wilted, don't buy them.

If you like your spring greens softly cooked, microwaved ones will not be to your liking. They have a firm texture – on the tough side if not absolutely fresh – and surprisingly the colour is not so good.

Remove all thick tough stalks, wash the leaves well, then cut across into shreds.

TO COOK Put 450g/1lb prepared spring greens in a large ovenproof glass bowl with 3 tablespoons water. Cover with cling film (plastic wrap), leaving a small gap for the steam to escape, and cook on full power for 8–9 minutes. Drain, season and serve.

• SQUASH OR LARGE ZUCCHINI •

See MARROW.

• STOCK •

A good stock is the foundation of the best home-made soups and is a means of enriching many sauces. Stocks are very easy to prepare and use skin and bones which would otherwise be discarded. Chicken and fish are the ones to make in a microwave. Beef is best left to conventional cooking as it needs long, gentle simmering to achieve a really rich flavour.

• FISH STOCK •

Wash about 450 g/1 lb white fish heads, bones and skin and put into a large ovenproof glass bowl with 750 ml/1¼ pints/1½ pints hot water. Add a chopped onion, salt, 6 peppercorns and a bouquet garni. Cover and cook on full power for about 10 minutes. Reduce to low power (30%) and cook for 10 minutes. Strain through a fine nylon sieve and use straight away or cool and refrigerate for up to 2 days. This gives you a good base for a fish soup. If you need a more concentrated flavour for a sauce, boil to reduce it a little.

• CHICKEN STOCK •

Break up a chicken carcass and put into a large ovenproof glass bowl. Add any chicken bones and skin that are available – they will enrich the flavour. Giblets, too, if you have them but not the liver. Add a washed, quartered but unpeeled (unpared) carrot, a halved onion, salt, a few peppercorns and a bouquet garni. Cover with 900 ml/1¼ pints/2 pints hot water and cook on full power for 15 minutes. Reduce to low power (30%) and cook for another 15 minutes. Stand for 15 minutes and strain. Leave until cold and remove the fat. You should have 450 ml/¾ pint/2 cups lightly jellied, well-flavoured stock.

• SWEDES (RUTABAGAS) •

Choose firm small swedes avoiding any damaged ones. Scrub and peel (pare) them thickly so that all the tough skin is removed. Cut into even-sized slices or small cubes.

TO COOK Put 450 g/1 lb cubed swede into a dish with 2 tablespoons water. Cover with cling film (plastic wrap), leaving a small gap for the steam to escape, and cook on full power for 10–12 minutes, stirring once. Drain, season and serve or mash with a little butter, season and serve.

• SWEETBREADS •

Calf's and lamb's sweetbreads, with their delicate flavour and creamy texture, are considered a delicacy with the former acknowledged as being the finest.

They need blanching before cooking and this is quickly done conventionally. Rinse them several times in cold water, then put into a pan, cover with cold water and bring to the boil. Boil for 2 minutes, drain and put into cold water to cool. Drain and dry them and remove as much of the membrane as possible. They are now ready for cooking.

TO COOK Put 450 g/1 lb prepared sweetbreads, cut into thick slices, in a dish with 150 ml/¼ pint/⅔ cup chicken stock and white wine or all stock. Cover with cling film (plastic wrap), leaving a small gap for the steam to escape, and cook on full power for 8–10 minutes, until tender. Transfer the sweetbreads to a plate, leaving the cooking liquor in the dish. Cook the liquor, uncovered, in the dish for 5–6 minutes until reduced to about half. Stir in 2–3 tablespoons thick (heavy) cream, season with salt and pepper and cook for 1 minute. Return the sweetbreads to the sauce and reheat for 2 minutes, or until heated through. Garnish with cooked mushrooms and sprinkle with freshly snipped (chopped) chives.

• SWEETCORN •

Fresh corn should be plump and full, with the kernels just turning yellow, the husks stiff and green. The husks and silky threads can be left on for microwaving but as they are hot to hold and steamy to strip off after cooking, it seems sensible to remove them first.

TO COOK Place 2 cobs on a dish with 2 tablespoons water. Cover with cling film (plastic wrap), leaving a small gap for the steam to escape, and cook on full power for 6–7 minutes, rearranging half-way through the cooking time. Stand for 3 minutes, drain and serve with butter, salt and pepper.

• SWEETS (CANDIES) •

It is much simpler to make sweets in the microwave because with no direct heat there is less danger of burning and no need to stir constantly. But the same care is needed when boiling sugar as in conventional cooking. You need large containers that can withstand the high temperatures and, because the containers get extremely hot, oven gloves are essential.

After boiling point has been reached, the temperatures rise very rapidly so you will need to keep checking to avoid overcooking. Use a sugar thermometer if you like but do not put it in the microwave.

See Preserves and Sweets chapter on pages 184–9.

• TOMATOES •

Tomatoes are available all the year round and though usually thought of in terms of salads, make a quickly cooked hot vegetable. Wash and dry the tomatoes and prick them if left whole so the skins do not burst, or halve them.

TO COOK Put 4 whole tomatoes in a dish, cover with cling film (plastic wrap), leaving a small gap for the steam to escape, and cook on full power for 2–3 minutes. Four halves will take about 1½ minutes. They can be sprinkled with a little grated cheese for extra flavour. Timing depends on the firmness of the tomato. Check half-way through and remove any that are ready as they will collapse if overcooked. The skins remain quite firm.

PEPERONATA

Tomatoes and (bell) peppers are cooked together to make a richly aromatic dish. Put 1 chopped large onion in a dish with 2 tablespoons oil and a crushed garlic clove. Cover with cling film (plastic wrap), leaving a small gap for the steam to escape, and cook on full power for 3 minutes. Cut 3 peppers (red are the sweetest) in halves, discard the seeds and pith (white membrane) and cut them into slices. Add to the onions and cook for 3 minutes. Peel and chop 450 g/1 lb tomatoes and add to the peppers. Cover and cook for 3 minutes. Stir, season with salt and freshly ground black pepper and cook uncovered for a further 8 minutes until the vegetables are soft and moist but with no surplus liquid.

Serve the peperonata with ham, sausages or eggs. When cold it makes a lovely first course accompanied by black olives and French bread.

• TONGUE •

Tongue needs long slow cooking in plenty of liquid to soften it and this is best done conventionally.

• TROUT •

Rainbow trout are now farmed on an extensive scale and available all the year round. They should be gutted (eviscerated), cleaned and served whole. They are usually fried or grilled (pan fried or broiled) but can be cooked in the microwave if you do not mind the soft skin. If sprinkled with toasted flaked almonds, this will be less apparent. Wash and dry the trout and slash the skin two or three times to prevent it bursting.

TO COOK Put 50 g/2 oz/¼ cup butter in a dish and heat on full power for 1 minute until melted. Put in 4 prepared trout (about 225 g/8 oz each), and turn them in the butter. Cover with cling film (plastic wrap), leaving a small gap for the steam to escape, and cook on full power for 8 minutes, turning and re-positioning half-way through the cooking. Shield the tails with small pieces of foil. Stand for 3 minutes. Sprinkle with toasted flaked almonds and serve with lemon wedges.

• TURKEY •

The size turkey you choose to cook in the microwave will obviously be governed by your oven capacity but it is best not to exceed one of about 5.5 kg/12 lb. Larger than this, it is more likely to cook unevenly and will be difficult to re-position.

Prepare in the same way as for conventional cooking. Put any stuffing into the neck cavity, fold the skin over it on to the bird and secure with wooden cocktail sticks (toothpicks). Tie or secure the legs and wings to the body. As turkey is a dry bird, brush over the surface with melted butter.

Either stand the turkey on a dish and completely cover with cling film (plastic wrap) or place it in a roasting bag and seal the ends loosely with an elastic band. Cook on full power, turning over three or four times.

TIMING about 6–7 minutes per 450 g/1 lb. Although a large turkey will colour, it will not crisp or be such a deep brown as a conventionally roasted bird, so you may like to complete the roasting in a hot oven (220 C, 425 F, gas 7) for about 20 minutes.

For more detailed instructions on cooking and special points to observe see CHICKEN and POULTRY.

• TURNIPS (WHITE TURNIPS) •

Keep winter or main-crop turnips for use in soups and stews but serve the young spring turnips with their white flesh and sweet flavour as a vegetable in their own right. Peel (pare) and cut the turnips into even-sized pieces.

TO COOK Put 450 g/1 lb prepared turnips in a dish with 3 tablespoons water. Cover with cling film, leaving a small gap for the steam to escape, and cook on full power for 10–12 minutes. Drain, add 1 tablespoon butter and let it melt over the turnips, season and serve.

• VEAL •

Veal is calves' meat and therefore is young and tender with a delicate flavour. It contains little fat. As veal is pale in colour even when conventionally cooked, the colouring achieved in the microwave is quite acceptable. But a short time in a hot oven will give it a more 'roasted' look.

TIMING about 7–9 minutes per 450 g/1 lb.

TO COOK Place a 1.25-kg/2½-lb cut of veal on a roasting rack and cover with a slit roasting bag. Cook on full power for 10 minutes, turn and cook for a further 10 minutes. Baste with the cooking juices and transfer to a moderately hot oven (200C, 400F, gas 6) for 10–15 minutes to 'roast' the surface.

Use the sediment and juices in the roasting tin (pan), adding chicken stock and/or white wine to make a light gravy.

• CHOPS •

These may be cooked in the microwave and are best browned in a browning dish or frying pan (skillet) if they are to be served plain.

• ESCALOPES •

These are cut from the leg of veal. They are a beautifully tender cut with no fat and are best lightly cooked and coated with a sauce. They can also be stuffed and rolled and cooked in, or served with, a creamy sauce.

See also MEAT.

• VEGETABLES •

Most vegetables cook beautifully in the microwave, often giving results which are superior to those achieved by conventional cooking. For the best results the vegetables must be absolutely fresh. This is particularly true of the brassica family – cabbage, Brussels sprouts and cauliflower – as if these are stale their taste can become unpleasantly strong when they are cooked with very little moisture.

Vegetables will cook more evenly if they are roughly the same size. This means choosing all small or all large whole vegetables like Brussels sprouts; if necessary halving large cauliflower florets and cutting root vegetables to the same thickness or into similar-sized chunks.

When cooked, vegetables will be firm but tender. Resist the temptation to continue cooking to soften them completely. The reverse happens: they dry out and harden and can end up inedible. If you like your vegetables very soft, cook them conventionally.

Vegetables retain their goodness, flavour and colour so well because they are cooked quickly and with the minimum of water. You may well find that with the consequent improvement in flavour, you can cut down on the salt when seasoning them.

In many cases the container you use can be the serving dish but with bulky vegetables, like shredded cabbage or spinach, you will need a large ovenproof bowl, a roasting bag or boiling bag.

Roasting and boiling bags come in several sizes and can be used for most vegetables. They are easy to use, just put in the prepared vegetables and water and fasten the top loosely with an elastic band. Where recipe instructions say 'stir', you just shake. Reservations about using them are that they are hot to handle and can be tricky to drain and for everyday use they are an extra expense. They can be re-used but this entails washing and drying them. Boiling bags are a little cheaper than roasting bags.

See under individual entries for full cooking instructions.

• VENISON •

Venison is the name given to the flesh of the deer. It is a dark, closely-grained meat with little fat and is rich and gamey if well hung. Like beef some cuts are more suitable for microwaving than others. The prime roasting cuts are the haunch and the loin, which can also be cut into chops. Shoulder is usually casseroled and is best cooked conventionally.

Marinating gives flavour and helps to tenderise the meat but is not essential. Venison is a dry meat and needs added fat to keep it moist. This can be done by larding it (pushing small pieces of fat into the flesh), or barding it (tying slices of fat over the surface).

Have the meat tied in a compact shape where possible and if it has no covering of fat, rub the surface with oil. Cook as beef (see page 46); it is at its best when under rather than overdone, so time it as for rare beef at 5–6 minutes per 450 g/1 lb.

The meat is naturally dark and if there is no fat round it that needs crisping, it need not be transferred to a hot oven. Just stand it under a tent of foil for 10–15 minutes to complete the cooking.

Make a good rich gravy using beef stock and red wine or a glass of port and stir in 1–2 teaspoons redcurrant jelly at the end.

• YORKSHIRE PUDDING •

This cannot be cooked in the microwave; it needs a hot oven to puff and crisp it.

• ZUCCHINI •

See COURGETTES.

R·E·C·I·P·E·S

◇ SOUPS ◇ AND STARTERS

TOMATO SOUP

◇ SERVES 4 ◇

- 25 g/1 oz/2 tablespoons butter
- 1 small onion, finely chopped
- 450 g/1 lb tomatoes, peeled and chopped
- 300 ml/½ pint/1¼ cups hot chicken stock
- salt and freshly ground black pepper
- 2 tablespoons concentrated tomato purée
- pinch of ground mace
- 4 tablespoons double (heavy) cream (optional)

Place the butter in an ovenproof bowl and melt in the microwave on full power for 1 minute. Add the onion and cook for 2 minutes. Stir in the tomatoes, then gradually add the chicken stock, seasoning, tomato purée and mace. Cook for 10 minutes. Allow to cool slightly, then sieve or blend to a purée. Serve in individual bowls with swirls of the cream, if liked.

• NOTE •

To peel (skin) tomatoes, place in a bowl and cover with boiling water. Leave for 30 to 60 seconds, then make a slit in the tomato skins with a sharp knife. The skins should peel away quite easily.

SPRING VEGETABLE SOUP

◇ SERVES 4–6 ◇

50 g/2 oz mange tout (snow peas)
1 onion, chopped
3 carrots, sliced
100 g/4 oz baby (white) turnips, diced
40 g/1½ oz/3 tablespoons butter
100 g/4 oz broccoli florets
2 courgettes (zucchini), sliced
1.15 litres/2 pints/5 cups hot chicken or vegetable stock
salt and freshly ground black pepper

Top and tail the mange tout and halve crosswise. Place the onion, carrot, turnip and butter in a large ovenproof bowl. Cover and cook on full power for 3 minutes. Add the remaining vegetables and 300 ml/½ pint/1¼ cups stock. Cook for 5 minutes. Top up the soup with the remaining stock and season to taste.

SERVING SUGGESTION

Crunchy hot herb bread, flavoured with the first of the season's fresh herbs, complements this light soup very well. Follow the instructions for making garlic bread (see page 72) but use about 4 tablespoons chopped fresh herbs to flavour the butter instead of the garlic. Select as many herbs as are available, using only small quantities of those which have a strong flavour. For example, thyme, parsley, marjoram, tarragon, chives and dill can all be used; add small quantities of rosemary and sage if you like.

CARROT AND ORANGE SOUP

◇ SERVES 4 ◇

Use this as a basic recipe for all cream of vegetable soups: cooking the vegetables in a small quantity of stock and using the remainder of the stock to thin the purée to taste. Use half stock and half milk for a creamier soup.

- 25 g/1 oz/2 tablespoons butter
- 1 small onion, chopped
- 450 g/1 lb carrots, thinly sliced
- 600 ml/1 pint/2½ cups hot light chicken stock
- 1 teaspoon sugar
- 6 tablespoons freshly squeezed orange juice
- salt and freshly ground pepper

Put the butter, onion, carrots, 150 ml/¼ pint/⅔ cup stock and the sugar in an ovenproof bowl, cover with cling film (plastic wrap), leaving a small gap for the steam to escape, and cook on full power for 10 to 14 minutes until the carrots are tender, stirring twice. Stir in the orange juice and blend or sieve to a smooth purée. Thin with the remaining stock to the desired consistency. Season to taste and reheat for 3 to 5 minutes, then serve hot with croûtons.

This also makes an excellent chilled soup with a rich, full flavour. Serve it cold with a spoonful of thick yogurt and a sprinkling of grated orange rind. Or grate a carrot and stir this in just prior to serving for a contrast in texture.

CUCUMBER AND YOGURT SOUP

◇ SERVES 4 ◇

A good home-made stock makes all the difference to this delicate and delicious soup. You'll find the recipe for a quickly made chicken stock on page 114.

- 1 small onion
- 25 g/1 oz/2 tablespoons butter
- 1 large cucumber
- 450 ml/¾ pint/2 cups hot chicken stock
- salt and pepper
- 2 teaspoons chopped fresh mint
- 150 ml/¼ pint/⅔ cup thick natural yogurt

Finely chop the onion, then place it in a large bowl with the butter and cook on full power for 2 minutes or until the onion has softened.

Peel the cucumber and cut it into small dice. Add to the onion, stirring it into the buttery juices with 150 ml/¼ pint/⅔ cup of the stock. Cover with cling film (plastic wrap), leaving a small gap for the steam to escape, and cook on full power for 10 minutes, stirring once, until the cucumber is tender.

Rub through a sieve or purée in a blender or food processor. Stir in remaining stock and season with salt and pepper. Leave until cool then cover and chill in the refrigerator.

Mix the mint into the yogurt then stir this into the soup just before serving and taste to check the seasoning.

TOMATO CHARTREUSE

◇ SERVES 4 ◇

300 ml/$\frac{1}{2}$ pint/1$\frac{1}{4}$ cups tomato juice
2 teaspoons powdered gelatine
4 tablespoons very finely diced raw vegetables (choose one or a mixture of celery, cucumber, fennel, red and green (bell) peppers)

Some tomato juices have more flavour than others, so check before you start and add a little more seasoning if necessary.

Put 3 tablespoons of the tomato juice into a small bowl. Sprinkle the gelatine over it and leave to soften for about 10 minutes. Dissolve the gelatine on full power for 15 to 30 seconds. Stir well to ensure it has completely dissolved. Cool the gelatine mixture slightly before stirring it into the rest of the tomato juice.

Cool until beginning to set then stir in the vegetables. Spoon into four individual ramekins (custard cups) and leave to set.

SERVING SUGGESTION

Serve these with brown bread and butter. As a change from slices, cut the bread thinly and trim off the crusts. Butter each slice then roll up Swiss roll fashion. Depending on the loaf size halve or quarter the slices to make tiny rolls which look more appetising. Two slices per person should be sufficient. If you prefer a crisp accompaniment a batch of the crispy garlic bread slices (see page 72) would be a good choice.

CRAB-STUFFED MUSHROOMS

◇ SERVES 4 ◇

4 large mushrooms
15 g/½ oz/1 tablespoon butter
2 tablespoons flour
150 ml/¼ pint/⅔ cup creamy milk
175 g/6 oz/¾ cup white crab meat
salt and pepper
juice of ½–1 lemon

Wipe the mushrooms, remove the stalks and place in a round dish. Chop the stalks and put into an ovenproof bowl with the butter. Cook on full power for 1 minute. Stir in the flour and cook for 30 seconds. Blend in the milk and cook for 2 to 3 minutes until boiling and thickened.

Cover the mushrooms with cling film (plastic wrap), leaving a small gap for the steam to escape, and cook for 3 minutes.

Stir the crab meat into the sauce and season with salt and pepper and plenty of lemon juice.

Drain the juices off the mushrooms. Heap the crab meat mixture on to the mushrooms and cook, uncovered, for 2 minutes.

Serve with fingers of hot, crisp toast or, if liked, sprinkle over crisp crumbs (see Tips page 36).

• VARIATION •

Canned tuna can be used to stuff the mushrooms instead of the crab. Drain and flake a 185-g/6½-oz can (about 1 cup canned) tuna and mix it with the sauce instead of the crab. Sprinkle the stuffed mushrooms with a little grated Parmesan cheese and some chopped parsley just before serving. To make a tasty supper dish double the quantities given above and serve the mushrooms with some warmed crusty bread.

HERBED CHICKEN LIVER PÂTÉ

◇ SERVES 6 ◇

450 g/1 lb chicken livers
50 g/2 oz/4 tablespoons butter
1 onion, chopped
1 teaspoon chopped fresh tarragon
1 teaspoon snipped (chopped) chives
1 teaspoon chopped parsley
salt and freshly ground black pepper

Trim, pat dry with kitchen paper and roughly chop the chicken livers, then place them in a large ovenproof bowl with 15 g/½ oz/1 tablespoon butter, the onion and herbs. Cover with cling film (plastic wrap) and cook on full power for 6 minutes, stirring twice. Blend the mixture in a food processor with the remaining butter and seasoning to taste. Spoon into small ramekins (custard cups) and chill thoroughly.

SERVING SUGGESTION

This light pâté can be served as a cocktail snack. Fit a medium-sized star pipe into a piping bag, then pipe the pâté on to tiny savoury biscuits, short strips of celery, slices of cucumber or small circles of crisp toast. Alternatively, pipe the pâté into scooped-out cherry tomatoes or use it to fill halved hard-boiled eggs. Cut the eggs in half and scoop out the yolks. Mash these with the pâté, then pipe the mixture back into the whites. Garnish the savouries with sprigs of parsley, halved stuffed olives or halved cucumber slices.

BROAD (FAVA OR LIMA) BEAN PÂTÉ

◇ SERVES 4 ◇

- 1 (275-g/10-oz) packet/2 cups frozen broad (fava or lima) beans
- 2 tablespoons water
- 50 g/2 oz/$\frac{1}{3}$ cup curd cheese
- salt and freshly ground pepper
- 1 tablespoon snipped (chopped) chives or summer savory

Put the beans into an ovenproof dish with the water, cover with cling film (plastic wrap), leaving a small gap for the steam to escape, and cook on full power for 8 minutes, or until tender. When cool enough to handle, pop the beans out of their skins. Purée them in a food processor together with the curd cheese. Season to taste with salt and pepper and stir in the chopped herbs. Spoon into a dish, cover and chill. Serve with toast or pitta bread.

SERVING SUGGESTION

In addition to crisp toast or pitta bread, you may like to serve some Parma ham with this pâté. Trim the ham and arrange the slices on a platter, leaving room for the dish of pâté in the middle. Add a few wedges of lemon so that the juices may be squeezed over the ham and serve with freshly ground black pepper.

SAVOURY CUSTARDS

◇ SERVES 4 ◇

These savoury custards can be filled with almost any vegetable or fish mixture. Think of them as quiches without the pastry and you'll appreciate the possibilities.

- 25 g/1 oz/2 tablespoons butter
- 4–6 spring onions (scallions), finely chopped
- 225 g/8 oz or 4 small courgettes (zucchini), grated
- 150 ml/¼ pint/⅔ cup milk
- 2 eggs, beaten
- salt and freshly ground pepper
- 3 tablespoons grated Parmesan cheese

Put the butter into an ovenproof bowl and melt on full power for 30 to 45 seconds. Stir in the onion and cook for 1 minute. Add the grated courgettes and cook for 2 minutes.

Pour the milk into a bowl and heat for 1 minute. Stir it into the beaten eggs and season with salt and pepper to taste. Stir in the courgettes and Parmesan cheese and divide the mixture between four ramekin dishes (custard cups). Stand the dishes in a large outer dish and half fill this with hot water. Cook, uncovered, for 3 to 4 minutes, then leave to stand for 3 minutes. The centres should be creamy and the whole custards softly rather than firmly set. Serve warm rather than hot.

◇ FISH ◇ AND SHELLFISH

FISH AND SPINACH PIE

◇ SERVES 4–6 ◇

• TOPPING •

1 kg/2 lb potatoes
4 tablespoons water
25 g/1 oz/2 tablespoons butter
5–6 tablespoons milk
salt and pepper

• SAUCE •

3 tablespoons flour
450 ml/¾ pint/2 cups milk
40 g/1½ oz/3 tablespoons butter
100 g/4 oz/1 cup Cheddar cheese, grated
pinch of mustard powder

• FILLING •

450 g/1 lb cod or haddock fillets
2 hard-boiled eggs
1 (290-g/10.6-oz) packet/about 2 cups frozen
cut-leaf spinach

Peel and dice the potatoes and put into a bowl with the water. Cover with cling film (plastic wrap), leaving a small gap for the steam to escape, and cook on full power for 12 to 14 minutes, or until the potatoes are soft. If preferred the potatoes can be cooked conventionally.

Put the flour for the sauce into a large jug (pitcher) and gradually stir in the milk. Dot the butter over the top and cook on full power for 3 minutes. Remove and stir well, blending the mixture together and leaving no lumps of flour in the base. Cook for 2 minutes, stir and cook for 1 minute, by which time the sauce should have boiled and thickened. Stir in the cheese and season with salt, pepper and mustard.

Arrange the fish fillets in a dish, placing the thinner parts towards the centre. Cover with cling film (plastic wrap), leaving a small gap for the steam to escape, and cook on full power for 4 minutes, rearranging once. Set aside.

Turn the spinach into a dish, cover with cling film, leaving a small gap for the steam to escape, and cook on full power for 4 minutes. Stir and cook for a further 5 minutes.

Whilst the spinach is cooking drain and mash the potatoes, beat in the butter and milk and season with salt and pepper.

Flake the fish into the sauce. Spoon this mixture into an 18-cm/7-in soufflé dish. Spoon the potato around the edge. Drain and season the spinach and spoon it into the middle. Cover loosely and reheat on full power for 3 to 5 minutes.

STUFFED COD CUTLETS

◇ SERVES 4 ◇

25 g/1 oz/2 tablespoons butter
1 small onion, finely chopped
4 rashers (slices) rindless bacon, chopped
2 tomatoes, chopped
25 g/1 oz/$\frac{1}{3}$ cup fresh breadcrumbs
4 cod cutlets (steaks), central bones removed
4 tablespoons milk
salt and freshly ground black pepper

Place the butter, onion and bacon in a small ovenproof bowl and cook on full power for 3 minutes. Add the tomatoes and breadcrumbs and mix well. Place the cod cutlets in a shallow, ovenproof dish and fill the centre of each cutlet with the stuffing mixture. Top each cutlet with a tablespoon of milk and season to taste. Cover with cling film (plastic wrap), allowing a small gap for the steam to escape, and cook for 5 minutes.

ORIENTAL FISH FILLETS

◇ SERVES 4 ◇

675 g/1½ lb cod or haddock fillets
3 spring onions (scallions)
1 (1-cm/½-in) cube fresh root ginger
1½ tablespoons sherry
1½ tablespoons soy sauce
1 teaspoon sugar

Wash and skin the fish and cut into four even-sized pieces. Cut the onions into small diagonal slices. Peel the ginger and cut into thin slices and then into slivers. Mix the sherry, soy sauce and sugar together.

Put half the ginger and onion in a dish and lay the fish fillets on top. Sprinkle over the remaining ginger and onion and the sherry mixture. Cover with cling film (plastic wrap), leaving a small gap for the steam to escape, and cook on full power for 6 minutes, rearranging once.

Serve with the juices spooned over the fish.

SERVING SUGGESTION

To accompany this dish you may like to cook some mange-tout peas or broccoli florets (see pages 84 and 52). Arrange the cooked vegetables in small bowls, sprinkle with a little light soy sauce and a few very fine strips of red (bell) pepper. In addition, cook some plain rice to complete the meal (see page 106).

FISH TERRINE

◇ SERVES 4–6 ◇

675 g/1½ lb cod, skinned and boned
2 tablespoons chopped fresh parsley, chives, tarragon and dill
50 g/2 oz/⅔ cup breadcrumbs
1 egg
juice of ½–1 lemon
salt and pepper
2 small smoked trout

Purée the cod in a food processor. Add the herbs and breadcrumbs. Stir in the beaten egg and season well with lemon juice, salt and pepper.

Skin and fillet the trout. Grease a 900-ml/1½-pint/3¾-cup ovenproof terrine, place half of the cod mixture on the bottom. Lay the trout fillets on top and cover with the remaining cod. Smooth over the surface.

Cover with cling film (plastic wrap), leaving a small gap for the steam to escape. Cook for 12 minutes, then leave to stand in the dish for 4 to 5 minutes before turning out. Serve hot or cold with Hollandaise Sauce (see page 179), if liked.

• VARIATION •

You may like to layer peeled cooked prawns (shrimps), which must be defrosted if frozen, in this terrine instead of the smoked trout. Alternatively, sliced scallops can be layered with the fish. Clean the scallops and cut them into thin slices, then lay these on top of the cod mixture. If you want to make the terrine particularly lavish, then use a mixture of scallops and prawns.

KEDGEREE

◇ SERVES 4–6 ◇

225 g/8 oz smoked haddock
2 kipper fillets
150 ml/¼ pint/⅔ cup water
40 g/1½ oz/3 tablespoons butter
1 onion, chopped
2 teaspoons curry paste or powder
225 g/8 oz/1 cup long-grain rice
½ teaspoon salt
rind and juice of 1 lemon
50 g/2 oz/¼ cup toasted split almonds (optional)
2 hard-boiled eggs, quartered
freshly ground black pepper

Place the fish in a shallow dish with the water. Cover with cling film (plastic wrap) and cook on full power for 5 minutes. Drain, reserving the stock and flake the fish, removing any skin and bones.

Place the butter and onion in a large ovenproof bowl. Cook for 2 minutes. Stir in the curry paste or powder, rice and salt. Make the fish stock up to 600 ml/1 pint/2½ cups with water and pour over. Cover and cook for 10 minutes. Stir in the fish, lemon rind and juice, almonds and eggs. Cook for a further 5 minutes. Fork up the rice and season with pepper before serving.

SERVING SUGGESTION

Traditionally, kedgeree is served for breakfast but it is also excellent for lunch or supper. For a change you may like to offer a bowl of soured cream sprinkled with a little grated lemon rind and parsley to accompany the kedgeree. A salad of finely sliced cucumber and chopped spring onions (scallions) complements kedgeree very well.

SEAFOOD PAELLA

◇ SERVES 4–6 ◇

- 4 tablespoons olive oil
- 1 onion, finely chopped
- 2 cloves garlic, crushed
- 1 red (bell) pepper, deseeded and chopped
- $\frac{1}{4}$ teaspoon saffron powder or ground saffron strands
- 450 ml/$\frac{3}{4}$ pint/2 cups hot chicken stock
- 225 g/8 oz/1 cup long-grain rice
- 1 boneless chicken breast, skinned
- 225 g/8 oz/1 cup peeled cooked prawns (shrimps)
- 100 g/4 oz/1 cup cooked mussels
- 100 g/4 oz/1$\frac{1}{2}$ cups frozen peas
- 3 tomatoes, peeled and chopped
- salt and freshly ground black pepper
- 2 tablespoons chopped parsley
- whole cooked prawns (shrimps) (optional) to garnish

Place the oil, onion, garlic and red pepper in a large ovenproof bowl and cook on full power for 5 minutes. Mix the saffron with 2 tablespoons of the stock, then add to the bowl with the remaining stock and the rice. Stir well, then add the chicken to the mixture. Cover with cling film (plastic wrap), allowing a small gap for the steam to escape, and cook for 10 minutes. Remove the chicken from the bowl and cut into pieces, then return to the bowl. Add the prawns, mussels, peas and tomatoes to the bowl and cook for a further 5 minutes. Season to taste and sprinkle with the chopped parsley. Serve hot, garnished with a few whole prawns, if wished.

CURRIED CHICKEN MOUSSE

◇ SERVES 4–6 ◇

- 1 tablespoon oil
- 1 small onion, finely chopped
- 1 tablespoon curry powder
- 150 ml/$\frac{1}{4}$ pint/$\frac{2}{3}$ cup hot chicken stock
- 350 g/12 oz/$\frac{3}{4}$ lb boneless chicken breasts
- salt and pepper
- lemon juice
- 3 teaspoons powdered gelatine
- 150 ml/$\frac{1}{4}$ pint/$\frac{2}{3}$ cup mayonnaise
- 1 tablespoon apricot purée or sieved apricot jam (jelly)
- 2 egg whites

Put the oil and onion in a dish and cook on full power for 1 to 2 minutes or until the onion has softened. Stir in the curry powder and cook for a further 30 seconds.

Measure 3 tablespoons of the stock into a small bowl. Stir the rest into the onion and curry mixture. Arrange the chicken breasts in the dish with the thickest parts to the outer edge. Cover with cling film (plastic wrap), leaving a small gap for the steam to escape, and cook on full power for 4 minutes rearranging half-way through the cooking. Allow to stand for 2 minutes, then check that the chicken is fully cooked. Blend the chicken pieces and the juices in a food processor or blender until smooth. Season with salt and pepper and a squeeze of lemon juice, then leave until cold.

Sprinkle the gelatine over the reserved stock, leave to soften for about 10 minutes, then dissolve on full power for 15 to 30 seconds. Stir until completely dissolved, leave to cool slightly, then stir it into the mayonnaise together with the apricot jam. Mix this into the cold chicken mixture and check the seasoning.

Whisk (beat) the egg whites and fold through the mixture, then spoon it into a 900-ml/1½-pint/2½-cup ring mould or loaf dish and leave to set.

SERVING SUGGESTION

This lightly curried mousse is particularly good with an orange and avocado salad. If in a ring mould, turn out on to a bed of shredded lettuce and fill the centre with the salad: peeled and diced avocado with segments of orange free of all pith and membrane, and tossed in an orange or lemon dressing. If the mousse is set in a loaf dish, turn it out on to a bed of shredded lettuce and arrange alternate slices of avocado and orange segments either side of the mousse, then sprinkle them with the dressing.

Serve with baby new potatoes or a rice salad.

CHICKEN CACCIATORE

◇ SERVES 4 ◇

- 1 tablespoon vegetable oil
- 1 large onion, chopped
- 1 medium green (bell) pepper, deseeded and chopped
- 1 clove garlic, crushed
- 4 boneless chicken breasts, skinned
- 1 (227-g/8-oz) can/1 cup canned tomatoes
- salt and freshly ground black pepper
- watercress sprigs to garnish

Place the oil, onion, pepper and garlic in an ovenproof dish or casserole and cook on full power for 5 minutes. Add the chicken breasts, tomatoes and seasoning to taste to the dish. Cover with cling film (plastic wrap), allowing a small gap for the steam to escape, and cook for 8 minutes, rearranging the chicken breasts after 4 minutes. Serve garnished with sprigs of watercress and accompanied by plain boiled rice.

CHICKEN IN RED WINE

◇ SERVES 4 ◇

4 chicken pieces, skinned
1 bouquet garni
2 cloves garlic, crushed
salt and freshly ground black pepper
450 ml/¾ pint/2 cups full-bodied red wine
100 g/4 oz/4 slices rindless streaky smoked bacon
12–16 pickling or button onions
225 g/8 oz button mushrooms
25 g/1 oz/2 tablespoons butter
20 g/¾ oz/3 tablespoons flour
1–2 tablespoons chopped parsley

Place the chicken in a large glass bowl. Place the bouquet garni, garlic and seasoning on top of the chicken and pour in the red wine. Leave in the refrigerator for 12 to 24 hours to marinate.

When the chicken is ready, chop the bacon roughly and place in a separate dish with the onions. Cover with cling film (plastic wrap) and cook on full power for 5 minutes. Add the chicken and marinade and cook for a further 12 minutes, rearranging the chicken pieces twice during cooking. Add the mushrooms and cook for 5 minutes more.

Drain the stock from the chicken and vegetables and transfer these to a serving dish. In another bowl, melt the butter in the microwave for 30 seconds. Stir in the flour then gradually add the stock. Cook for 2 minutes, stirring once during cooking. Adjust the seasoning, stir in the parsley and pour over the chicken. Serve immediately.

SERVING SUGGESTION

This classic chicken casserole can be served with buttered noodles and a simple green salad. Cook the noodles (see page 94) before preparing the casserole, drain them and transfer to a microwave-proof serving dish. Top with a knob of butter and cover with cling film. When the chicken is ready reheat the noodles for 2 to 3 minutes before serving.

SPICY TOMATO CHICKEN

◇ SERVES 4 ◇

- 4 (225-g/8-oz) chicken pieces, skinned
- 1 small onion, finely chopped
- 1 tablespoon oil
- 2 tablespoons demerara sugar
- 1 tablespoon lemon juice
- 150 ml/¼ pint/⅔ cup tomato ketchup (catsup)
- 1 tablespoon Worcestershire Sauce
- 4 tablespoons water

Arrange the chicken pieces in an ovenproof dish in which they will fit with just enough room for the sauce. Make two cuts in the thickest part of each piece so the sauce can flavour the chicken.

Put the onion and oil in an ovenproof bowl, cover with cling film (plastic wrap), leaving a small gap for the steam to escape, and cook on full power for 2 minutes. Stir in the remaining ingredients, cover and cook for 4 minutes. Stir and pour over the chicken. Cover and cook for 10 minutes, rearrange and spoon the sauce over the chicken. Cook for 5 minutes, then allow to stand for 3 minutes. Serve with rice.

TURKEY ROULADES

◇ SERVES 4 ◇

- 4 (100-g/4-oz) turkey breast fillets
- 1 tablespoon oil
- 1 small onion, finely chopped
- 1 celery stalk, finely chopped
- 100 g/4 oz mushrooms, chopped
- 4 tablespoons fresh breadcrumbs
- salt and freshly ground pepper
- 4 tablespoons chicken stock
- 6 tablespoons natural chestnut purée (about 100 g/4 oz)
- 3 tablespoons single (light) cream

Put the breast fillets between two pieces of cling film (plastic wrap) and beat out to about 5 mm/$\frac{1}{4}$ in thickness.

Put the oil, onion and celery into an ovenproof bowl, cover with cling film (plastic wrap), leaving a small gap for the steam to escape, and cook on full power for 2 minutes. Add the mushrooms and cook for a further 2 minutes. Stir in the breadcrumbs and season to taste with salt and pepper.

Divide this stuffing between the four fillets, roll up and secure with a cocktail stick (wooden toothpick) and arrange round the outer edge of a dish.

Pour over the chicken stock, cover with cling film (plastic wrap), leaving a small gap for the steam to escape, and cook on full power for 4 minutes. Rearrange and cook for a further 2 minutes. Remove the cocktail sticks (toothpicks).

Put the chestnut purée into a bowl and stir in the juices from the meat together with the cream. Season to taste with salt and pepper and heat on full power for 2 minutes. Pour the sauce over the turkey roulades and serve immediately.

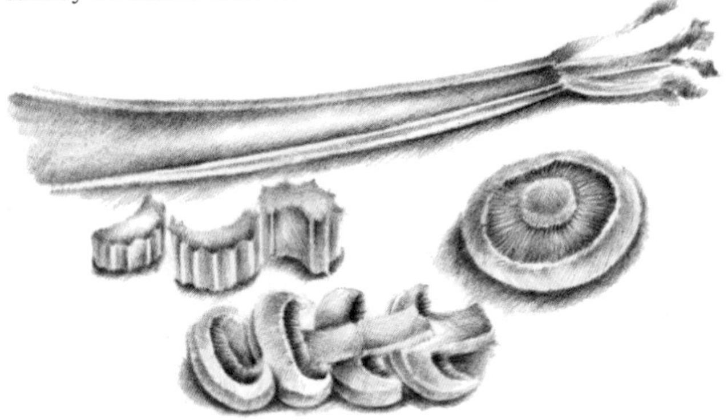

SERVING SUGGESTION

Serve some cooked rice flavoured with herbs to accompany the turkey. Cook the rice according to the instructions on page 106, adding 2–4 tablespoons chopped fresh herbs and a large knob of butter when you fluff up the grains. Try a mixture of herbs (parsley, thyme and chives, for example) or use one herb, for example parsley, tarragon, chives or thyme.

DUCK WITH APRICOT SAUCE

◇ SERVES 4 ◇

4 (275-g/10-oz) duck pieces
1 (411-g/14½-oz) can/2 cups canned apricot halves
150 ml/¼ pint/⅔ cup chicken stock
and white wine or all stock
1–2 tablespoons apricot brandy or brandy (optional)
2 teaspoons sugar
salt and freshly ground black pepper
1 teaspoon arrowroot
juice of ½ orange

Trim the duck pieces of any surplus fat and prick the skin well. Place on a rack, skin side down, cover with absorbent kitchen paper and cook on full power for 10 minutes. Drain off the fat and juices. Turn the pieces over and cook for a further 10 minutes.

Allow to stand for 5 minutes then grill (broil) until crisp and brown, or transfer the duck to a hot oven (230C, 450F, gas 8) for 10 to 15 minutes.

While the duck finishes cooking make the sauce. Drain the apricots and set 4 halves aside for garnish. Put the remainder in an ovenproof dish with the stock and wine, cover with cling film (plastic wrap), leaving a small gap for the steam to escape, and cook for 3 minutes. Turn the contents of the dish into a food processor or blender and purée. Add the brandy, if using, and season with sugar, salt and pepper.

Blend the arrowroot with the orange juice, stir into the purée, turn into a bowl and cook for 1 to 2 minutes to thicken and reheat the sauce.

Arrange the duck on a dish, topping each piece with an apricot half. Spoon a little of the sauce over and serve the rest separately.

◇ MEAT ◇ AND OFFAL

SAVOURY MEATLOAF

◇ SERVES 4 ◇

1 tablespoon oil
1 large onion, chopped
225 g/8 oz minced or ground beef
225 g/8 oz minced or ground pork
6 tablespoons fresh brown breadcrumbs
1 clove garlic, crushed
1 tablespoons concentrated tomato purée
salt and freshly ground black pepper
1 egg, beaten

Place the oil in a large ovenproof bowl with the onion and cook on full power for 3 minutes, stirring once. Stir in the meat, breadcrumbs, garlic and tomato purée. Season with salt and black pepper then stir in the beaten egg. Mix well and press into a 750-ml/$1\frac{1}{4}$-pint/3-cup ovenproof loaf dish or terrine (bread pan). Cook for 5 minutes, turning the dish twice during cooking. Remove from the microwave and wrap completely in aluminium foil, placing the shiny side of foil inwards, and leave to rest for 15 minutes. Remove the foil and return to the microwave for a further 3 minutes, then wrap in foil, as before, rest for 5 minutes. Serve cold with a mixed salad and crisp toast.

CHILLI CON CARNE

◇ SERVES 4 ◇

- 1 large onion, chopped
- 1 large green (bell) pepper, deseeded and chopped
- 100 g/4 oz mushrooms, sliced
- 3 tablespoons oil
- 2 cloves garlic, crushed
- 450 g/1 lb lean minced or ground beef
- 1–2 teaspoons chilli powder
- salt and freshly ground black pepper
- 1 (397-g/14-oz) can/2 cups canned chopped tomatoes
- 2 tablespoons concentrated tomato purée
- 1 (425-g/15-oz) can/1½ cups canned red kidney beans, drained

Place the onion, pepper and mushrooms in a large ovenproof bowl or suitable serving dish. Stir in the oil and garlic. Cover with cling film (plastic wrap), allowing a small gap for the steam to escape, and cook on full power for 7 minutes.

Stir the minced or ground beef into the onion mixture, making sure it is well broken up. Stir in the chilli powder, seasoning, tomatoes and tomato purée. Stir well, then re-cover the bowl and cook the chilli for a further 10 minutes. Stir in the kidney beans and cook for a further 5 minutes. Serve the chilli at once with plain boiled rice or baked potatoes.

SERVING SUGGESTION

Arrange a ring of shredded crisp lettuce (for example Iceberg) and chopped tomato round the edge of four individual plates, then ladle the chilli into the middle. Serve cooked rice or warmed French bread with the chilli and remember to offer a simple oil and vinegar salad dressing to go with the salad ingredients. This dressing can be flavoured with some finely chopped spring onion if you like.

SURPRISE STUFFED BEEF

◇ SERVES 4 ◇

575 g/1¼ lb minced or ground beef
50 g/2 oz/⅔ cup fresh breadcrumbs
1 medium onion, finely chopped
salt and pepper
1 egg, beaten
1 (283-g/10-oz) packet/about 2 cups frozen
stir-fried vegetables

• TOPPING •

2 tablespoons tomato ketchup (catsup)
1 tablespoon Worcestershire sauce
¼ teaspoon mustard powder

Mix the beef, breadcrumbs and onion together, season with salt and pepper and bind with the egg.

Line a 23-cm/9-in flan dish (pie pan), 3.5 cm/1½ in deep, with about three-quarters of the meat mixture.

Turn the frozen vegetables into an ovenproof bowl, cover with cling film (plastic wrap), leaving a small gap for the steam to escape, and cook on full power for 2 minutes. Drain well and pat dry. Spread over the meat base.

Take a sheet of cling film (plastic wrap) and press the remaining meat into a circle large enough to cover the top of the pie. Take it right up to the edge of the dish and quickly turn it over the filling. Remove the cling film (plastic wrap) and press the meat down to seal round the edges.

Mix the topping ingredients together and spoon over the pie. Leave uncovered and cook on full power for 12 minutes. Stand for 5 minutes, covered, before serving.

SERVING SUGGESTION

To make a flavoursome, satisfying family meal, try serving Courgettes with Tomatoes (see page 63) and Baked Potatoes (see page 100) with this unusual mince recipe.

LAMB IN DILL SAUCE

◇ SERVES 4 ◇

675 g/1½ lb lamb fillet (steaks)
2 carrots, sliced
1 small onion, finely chopped
2 stalks celery, sliced
2 tablespoons oil
2 tablespoons flour
300 ml/½ pint/1¼ cups chicken or lamb stock
½ teaspoon sugar
1 teaspoon vinegar
2 tablespoons single (light) cream
2 teaspoons dried dill weed or
1 tablespoon chopped fresh dill
salt and freshly ground pepper

Trim the lamb and cut into small cubes.

Put the carrot, onion and celery in a casserole or large ovenproof bowl with the oil. Cover with cling film (plastic wrap), leaving a small gap for the steam to escape, and cook on full power for 5 minutes.

Stir in the flour then the stock to make a smooth sauce. Add the meat, cover and cook for 15 minutes, stirring once. Stir in the sugar, vinegar, cream and dill. Season to taste with salt and pepper. Cook for a further 5 minutes, then stand for 5 minutes. Serve immediately.

• VARIATION •

Dried or fresh tarragon can be used instead of the dill in this recipe. Alternatively, rosemary is another herb which complements lamb. When fresh mint is available, sprinkle a little over new potatoes (see page 101 for cooking instructions) to serve with the lamb flavoured with dill.

LAMB MEATBALLS IN GREEN PEA SAUCE

◇ SERVES 4 ◇

Vegetables which are cooked, puréed then thinned with a little cream or milk make excellent sauces for all kinds of meat, poultry and fish. Spinach would also be good made into a sauce for these lamb meatballs.

• GREEN PEA SAUCE •

225 g/8 oz/3 cups frozen peas
2 tablespoons water
salt and pepper
5 tablespoons thin (light) cream or creamy milk

• MEATBALLS •

450 g/1 lb minced (ground) lamb
1 small onion, finely chopped
1 clove garlic, crushed
1 slice bread, crusts removed
salt and pepper
1 egg, beaten
1 tablespoon oil

Make the sauce first: turn the peas into a dish with the water. Cover with cling film (plastic wrap), leaving a small gap for the steam to escape, and cook for 5 minutes on full power, stirring once. Drain and purée the peas, season with salt and pepper and stir in the cream to give the right consistency for a sauce.

Place the lamb, onion and garlic in a bowl, crumble the bread into it, season with salt and pepper and mix together well. Bind with the beaten egg and shape into 16 meatballs.

Heat a browning dish according to the manufacturer's instructions, adding the oil for the last 30 seconds. Put the meatballs into the dish, shaking and turning them for a few seconds to colour them evenly. Cover and cook on full power for 7 minutes, stirring and rearranging once. Stand for 2 minutes. Meanwhile reheat the sauce for about 2 minutes.

Strain any fat and juices off the meatballs and pour the sauce over them.

BOBOTIE

◇ SERVES 4 ◇

1 thick slice bread, crusts removed
150 ml/¼ pint/⅔ cup milk
1 onion, chopped
1 dessert (eating) apple, cored and diced
1 tablespoon vegetable oil
2–3 teaspoons curry paste or powder
450 g/1 lb cooked, minced or ground lamb
15 g/½ oz/1 tablespoon raisins
15 g/½ oz/1 tablespoon blanched
almonds, roughly chopped
100 g/4 oz/⅔ cup cream cheese
2 eggs, lightly beaten
salt and freshly ground black pepper

Crumble the bread into the milk and leave to soak while preparing the remaining ingredients.

Place the onion, apple, oil and curry paste or powder in a 1.1-litre/2-pint/5-cup ovenproof casserole dish. Cover with cling film (plastic wrap) and cook on full power for 2 minutes. Stir in the lamb, raisins and almonds. Squeeze the bread dry and fork into the meat mixture with seasoning to taste.

To make the topping, blend the cream cheese with the beaten eggs, then gradually add the milk. Season well and pour gently over the meat mixture. Cook for 15 minutes. Allow to stand for 5 minutes, then serve.

SERVING SUGGESTION

Delicately flavoured basmati rice perfectly complements this curry-spiced dish. Instructions for cooking rice are given on page 106. If you like, add a contrast in texture to the menu by preparing a simple salad of tomatoes and finely sliced onion with some crunchy croûtons sprinkled over just before serving. The croûtons can be prepared in the microwave following the instructions given on page 36.

PORK CHOPS IN ORANGE SAUCE

◇ SERVES 4 ◇

- 1 tablespoon vegetable oil
- 1 small onion, finely chopped
- 2 tablespoons flour
- 300 ml/½ pint/1¼ cups chicken stock
- rind and juice of 1 orange
- 1 teaspoon concentrated tomato purée
- 1 teaspoon soft light brown sugar
- salt and freshly ground black pepper
- 4 pork chops

Place the oil and onion in an ovenproof bowl. Cover with cling film (plastic wrap), leaving a small gap for the steam to escape, and cook on full power for 2 minutes. Stir the flour into the onion mixture then gradually blend in the stock. Add the orange rind and juice, tomato purée and sugar and season well. Cook for 3 minutes, stirring twice during cooking.

Arrange the pork chops as far apart as possible in a shallow ovenproof dish. Pour the sauce over and cover with cling film (plastic wrap), leaving a small gap for the steam to escape. Cook for 12 minutes, turning the chops over once during cooking.

SERVING SUGGESTION

Prepare some Creamed Potatoes (see page 101) and allow them to cool slightly. Using a large potato nozzle, fitted in a large piping bag, pipe swirls of potato round the edge of a flameproof gratin dish. Place under a hot grill to brown and crisp the top. Arrange the pork chops, overlapping, in the middle of the dish and spoon the sauce over them. Garnish with slices of orange and watercress.

LIVER, BACON AND PRUNE CASSEROLE

◇ SERVES 4 ◇

- 100 g/4 oz/⅔ cup moisturised prunes
- 300 ml/½ pint/1¼ cups white wine or dry (apple) cider
- 1 small onion, chopped
- 2 medium leeks, thickly sliced
- 3 tablespoons oil
- 450 g/1 lb lamb's liver
- 300 ml/½ pint/1¼ cups hot chicken stock
- 2 tomatoes, quartered
- 2 teaspoons concentrated tomato purée
- salt and freshly ground black pepper
- 225 g/8 oz/8 slices streaky (Canadian) bacon

Place the prunes and wine, or cider, in a small ovenproof bowl and cook on full power for 10 minutes, stirring twice. In a separate bowl, mix the onion, leeks and oil and cook for 5 minutes. Cut the liver into slices and place in the bowl with the stock, tomatoes, tomato purée and seasoning.

Add the reserved prunes with their liquid. Roll up the bacon and add to the dish. Cover with cling film (plastic wrap), allowing a small gap for the steam to escape, and cook for 10 minutes, stirring once during this time.

DEVILLED KIDNEYS

◇ SERVES 4 ◇

- 1 onion, chopped
- 50 g/2 oz/4 tablespoons butter
- 450 g/1 lb lambs' kidneys, cored and chopped
- 1 tablespoon wholegrain mustard
- 1 tablespoon Worcestershire sauce
- dash of Tabasco sauce
- 3 tablespoons beef or lamb stock
- salt and freshly ground black pepper

Place the onion and butter in a large ovenproof bowl. Cover with cling film (plastic wrap) and cook on full power for 2 minutes. Stir in the remaining ingredients and cook for 10 minutes, stirring twice. Season to taste with salt and pepper and serve immediately.

SERVING SUGGESTION

For a light, tasty supper dish, serve these devilled kidneys with warmed bread and butter. If you want to make a meal of them, then spoon them on to a bed of cooked rice (see page 106) or pasta (see page 94). A simple green salad can be served with the kidneys.

BRAISED FENNEL

SERVES 4

- 2 bulbs of fennel
- 6 tomatoes, peeled and sliced
- 6 tablespoons dry white wine
- 6 tablespoons chicken stock
- 2 tablespoons concentrated tomato purée
- salt and freshly ground black pepper

Trim and halve the fennel, reserving any feathery leaves for a garnish. In a shallow ovenproof dish make a bed of tomato slices. Place the fennel on top. Mix together the wine, stock and tomato purée and pour over the fennel. Season with salt and pepper.

Cover with cling film (plastic wrap), leaving a small gap for the steam to escape, and cook on full power for 12 minutes. Serve garnished with the reserved fennel leaves.

VARIATION

To make a simple supper dish, sprinkle a mixture of fresh breadcrumbs and grated cheese over the cooked fennel to make a thick coating and brown the top under a hot grill. Serve at once.

CARROT PURÉE

◇ SERVES 4 ◇

As a change from crisply cooked vegetables serve them softly puréed. Cauliflower, Brussels sprouts, parsnips and peas all make delicious purées. Cook them until tender, adding a little more stock or water than usual.

- 450 g/1 lb carrots, thinly sliced
- 5 tablespoons chicken stock or water
- 25 g/1 oz/2 tablespoons butter
- 4 tablespoons single (light) cream
- salt and pepper

Place the carrots and stock or water in an ovenproof dish, cover with cling film (plastic wrap), leaving a small gap for the steam to escape, and cook on full power for 8 to 9 minutes, stirring twice.

Drain and purée in a food processor with the butter and cream. Season to taste with salt and pepper.

Spoon into a serving dish and reheat, if necessary, for 1 to 2 minutes.

SERVING SUGGESTION

Puréed vegetables can be spooned into a serving dish, on to rounds of fried bread (large croûtons) or served in crisp pastry cases. Alternatively, the purée can be spread in a warmed shallow serving dish and used as a base for serving fish steaks, chops or chicken portions, kebabs or sausages. Small portions of the purée can be spooned on to individual plates, then topped attractively with a single serving of the main dish.

SCALLOPED ARTICHOKES

◇ SERVES 4 ◇

675 g/1½ lb Jerusalem artichokes
25 g/1 oz/2 tablespoons butter
salt and pepper
150 ml/¼ pint/⅔ cup single (light) cream or milk
½ teaspoon flour

Peel (pare) the artichokes and drop immediately into salted water so that they do not discolour. There should be about 450 g/1 lb when prepared.

Use the butter to grease a 20-cm/8-in round shallow dish. Drain the artichokes, slice them thinly and layer into the dish, seasoning with salt and pepper. Pour over the cream or milk mixed with the flour – this helps to prevent it separating. Cover with cling film (plastic wrap), leaving a small gap for the steam to escape, and cook on full power for 8 to 9 minutes, until tender.

Brown the top by placing under the grill (broiler) for a few minutes.

• VARIATION •

Cut some cooked ham into fine strips and layer it with the sliced artichokes. Cook as above, then sprinkle with a little finely grated Gruyère or Emmental cheese before browning under the grill. Serve hot with crisp toast or crusty bread to make a delicious supper dish.

RATATOUILLE

◇ SERVES 4–6 ◇

- 450 g/1 lb aubergines (eggplant)
- salt and freshly ground black pepper
- 1 red (bell) pepper
- 1 large onion, chopped
- 2 cloves garlic, crushed
- 2 tablespoons olive oil
- 450 g/1 lb firm, ripe tomatoes
- 225 g/8 oz courgettes (zucchini)
- 3 tablespoons chopped parsley
- a little lemon juice

Trim the ends off the aubergines, then cut into chunks. Place these in a colander or sieve and sprinkle generously with salt. Set aside for 30 minutes, then rinse thoroughly and dry on absorbent kitchen paper.

While the aubergines are soaking, prepare the other ingredients. Trim the stalk off the pepper and remove all the seeds and pith from inside. Cut the pepper into strips. Place the onion in a large, ovenproof serving bowl with the pepper, garlic, aubergines and oil. Cover with cling film (plastic wrap) and cook on full power for 8 minutes.

While the aubergines are cooking, peel and quarter the tomatoes and slice the courgettes. Add these ingredients to the bowl. Cook for 7 minutes. Stir in the parsley, seasoning and lemon juice to taste. Serve immediately or chill.

SERVING SUGGESTION

Cook some pasta shapes (see page 94) and place them in the base of a flameproof dish. Ladle the ratatouille over the top to cover the pasta completely. Sprinkle a layer of grated Parmesan cheese and breadcrumbs over the top and dot with a little butter. Place under a hot grill (broiler) until crisp and golden, then serve immediately for lunch or supper. This pasta and ratatouille gratin can also be prepared and served in individual dishes.

STIR-FRIED VEGETABLES

◇ SERVES 4 ◇

15 g/½ oz/1 tablespoon butter
450 g/1 lb mixed prepared vegetables (chosen from cauliflower or broccoli florets, mange-tout (snow) peas, carrot cut into sticks, mushrooms, courgettes (zucchini), and spring onions (scallions), all sliced, and dwarf (green or snap) beans
1 tablespoon soy sauce

Preheat a browning dish according to the manufacturer's instructions. Add the butter for the last 30 seconds. Stir in the prepared vegetables, cover with cling film (plastic wrap), leaving a small gap for the steam to escape, and cook on full power for 4 minutes, stirring once.

Season with soy sauce and serve immediately.

SERVING SUGGESTIONS

The stir-fried vegetables make a crunchy filling for a plain omelette (see page 91). They can also be used as a topping for Baked Potatoes (see page 100) or arranged on a dish of scrambled eggs (see page 68) and topped with some chopped cooked bacon (see page 44).

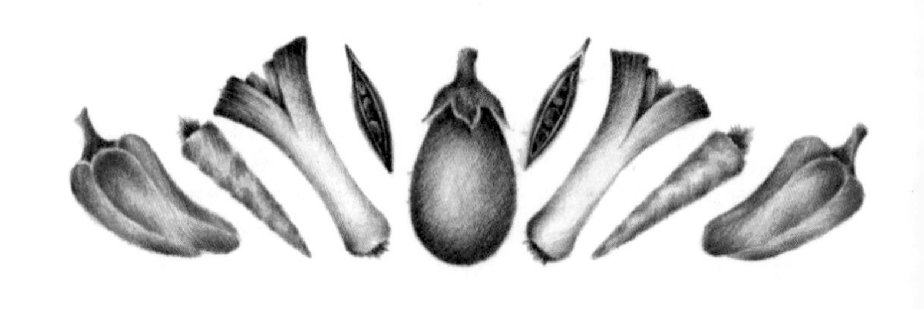

STUFFED MARROW RINGS

◇ SERVES 4 ◇

4 (3.5-cm/1½-in) thick slices marrow (squash)
(about 675 g/1½ lb in weight)
1 large onion, chopped
50 g/2 oz/¼ cup butter
225 g/8 oz/1⅓ cups lentils
300 ml/½ pint/1¼ cups boiling water
salt and freshly ground black pepper
1 teaspoon dried mixed herbs
1 (397-g/14-oz) can/2 cups canned chopped tomatoes
2 tablespoons creamed horseradish

• GARNISH •

lemon wedges and slices
parsley sprigs

Peel the marrow rings and hollow out the seeds and soft fibrous flesh which surrounds them to leave neat rings.

Place the onion and half the butter in a bowl (about 1.15-litre/2-pint/2½-pint capacity, but no smaller) and cook on full power for 3 minutes. Add the lentils and pour in the boiling water. Stir in seasoning to taste, the herbs and tomatoes, then cover with cling film (plastic wrap), allowing a small gap for the steam to escape. Cook for 15 minutes, by which time the lentils should be tender but still retain their shape.

Beat in the horseradish and remaining butter, taste and add more seasoning if necessary. Arrange the marrow rings as far apart as possible in a shallow dish. Cover with cling film (plastic wrap) and cook for 7 to 8 minutes. Pile the lentil mixture into the rings, mounding it on top so that they are almost completely covered. Cook for 2 minutes, then garnish with lemon wedges and slices and parsley, arranged beside the marrow rings, and serve.

SUPPER DISHES

TUNA AND RICE CASSEROLE

SERVES 4

1 onion, chopped
1 green (bell) pepper, deseeded and chopped
10C g/4 oz button mushrooms, sliced
2 tablespoons vegetable oil
100 g/4 oz/$\frac{1}{2}$ cup long-grain rice
1 (425-g/15-oz) can/2 cups canned mushroom soup
300 ml/$\frac{1}{2}$ pint/$1\frac{1}{4}$ cups chicken stock
2 (185-g/$6\frac{1}{2}$-oz) can/about 1 cup canned
tuna chunks in brine
freshly ground black pepper

Place the onion, pepper, mushrooms and oil in an ovenproof bowl. Cover with cling film (plastic wrap), leaving a small gap for the steam to escape, and cook on full power for 3 minutes. Stir in the rice, soup and stock. Cook for 12 minutes, stirring twice during cooking. Drain the tuna fish and stir into the rice mixture with pepper to taste. Cook for a further 2 minutes. Serve immediately.

SEAFOOD LASAGNE

◇ SERVES 4–6 ◇

225 g/8 oz lasagne
1.15 litres/2 pints/5 cups boiling water
2 tablespoons vegetable oil
450 g/1 lb haddock
225 g/8 oz scallops
300 ml/½ pint/1¼ cups dry white wine
6 black peppercorns
2 onions, 1 quartered and 1 chopped
2 bay leaves
50 g/2 oz/4 tablespoons butter
40 g/1½ oz/6 tablespoons flour
300 ml/½ pint/1¼ cups milk
100 g/4 oz/¾ cup peeled cooked prawns (shrimps)
2 tablespoons grated Parmesan cheese

Place the lasagne in a large ovenproof bowl and pour over the water and oil. Cover with cling film (plastic wrap) and cook on full power for 5 minutes, stirring once. Leave to stand for 10 minutes, then drain.

Place the haddock and scallops in a large ovenproof dish with the wine, peppercorns, the quartered onion and bay leaves. Cover and cook for 6 minutes. Drain and reserve the stock. Skin and flake the haddock and halve the scallops.

Place the chopped onion and butter in another bowl and cook for 2 minutes. Gradually blend in the flour, fish stock and milk. Cook for 8 minutes, whisking twice during the cooking time. Stir the haddock, scallops and prawns into three-quarters of the sauce. Layer in a shallow ovenproof dish with the sheets of lasagne, finishing with a layer of pasta. Finally, pour over the plain sauce and sprinkle with the Parmesan. Return to the microwave for 5 minutes to heat through. If liked, the lasagne can be popped under a hot grill (broiler) to brown the topping.

CHICKEN LIVERS WITH BULGAR

◇ SERVES 4 ◇

- 225 g/8 oz/1¼ cups bulgar (cracked wheat)
- 600 ml/1 pint/2½ cups hot chicken stock
- 2 onions, chopped
- 50 g/2 oz/4 tablespoons butter
- 450 g/1 lb chicken livers, roughly chopped
- 3 tablespoons white wine
- 3 tablespoons chicken stock
- 2 tablespoons chopped parsley
- 50 g/2 oz/½ cup button mushrooms, sliced
- 1 small red (bell) pepper, deseeded and diced
- 1 small green (bell) pepper, deseeded and diced
- salt and freshly ground black pepper
- chopped parsley to garnish

Soak the wheat in the chicken stock for 2 hours, adding extra liquid if required.

Place one chopped onion and half the butter in a bowl, cover and cook on full power for 2 minutes. Add the chicken livers, wine, stock and parsley. Cook for 6 minutes, stirring once during the cooking time. Season to taste.

Place the remaining butter and onion in a serving bowl, add the mushrooms and peppers, cover and cook for 3 minutes. Lightly drain the wheat and stir into the vegetables. Season to taste with salt and pepper and cook for 5 minutes. Make a hollow in the centre of the wheat and spoon in the chicken liver mixture. Cook for a further 2 minutes. Serve garnished with chopped parsley.

SCRAMBLED EGGS WITH RED PEPPER

◇ SERVES 2 ◇

1 onion, chopped
1 red (bell) pepper, deseeded and chopped
25 g/1 oz/2 tablespoons butter
4 eggs
2 tablespoons milk
salt and freshly ground black pepper

Cook the onion and pepper with the butter on full power for 4 minutes.

Whisk the eggs thoroughly with the milk and season to taste with salt and pepper. Add the vegetables to the eggs and mix well. Cook for 2 minutes, then whisk the eggs again thoroughly. Cook for a further minute and whisk again. Cook for a final minute and whisk again before serving. Serve at once with freshly made brown toast.

• VARIATIONS •

◇ Scrambled Eggs with Tomato Cook the onion as above but omit the red (bell) pepper. Peel and chop 4 medium tomatoes and add to the egg half-way through cooking.

◇ Scrambled Eggs with Prawns (Shrimps) Prepare the eggs and pepper as above. When the eggs are just beginning to set, add some peeled cooked prawns (defrosted if frozen) and continue cooking.

◇ Scrambled Eggs with Ham Add chopped cooked ham to the onion and pepper mixture with the beaten eggs. Cook as above.

CHEESE FONDUE

◇ SERVES 4 ◇

- 1 clove garlic
- 150 ml/$\frac{1}{4}$ pint dry white wine
- 450 g/1 lb Gruyère cheese, grated
- 1 tablespoon cornflour (cornstarch)
- 2 tablespoons Kirsch or gin

Peel and halve the garlic clove, then rub around the inside of the fondue pot – not a metal one or one which has a metal trim. You can use an attractive microwave-proof serving bowl of any type. Pour in the wine and cook on full power for 4 minutes.

Meanwhile, mix the cheese with the cornflour, making sure all the shreds are well coated. Beat half the cheese into the hot wine and cook for 2 minutes, then beat in the remaining cheese. Cook for a further 2 minutes. Add the Kirsch or gin and give the fondue a good beating, then cook for a final 4 minutes.

Place the bowl over a fondue burner or candle plate warmer and keep hot so that everybody can help themselves from the bowl.

SERVING SUGGESTION

The traditional accompaniment for fondue is crusty French bread, cut into cubes. These are speared on fondue forks and dipped into the hot cheese. However, in addition to bread, you may like to offer chunks of apple and celery, pieces of red and green (bell) pepper or crisp cocktail sausages with the fondue. If your guests are likely to be very hungry, then make a salad too – rice or pasta salad goes well with a cheese fondue.

BAKED POTATOES

◇ SERVES 4 ◇

4 medium potatoes

Prick the potatoes with a fork or knife to prevent them bursting during cooking. Cook on full power for 10 minutes. While they are cooking, prepare one of the fillings. Each of which will fill four potatoes.

• NOTE •

If liked, you can finish off the potatoes under a hot grill (broiler) for a few minutes. Brush the potatoes with a little oil or melted butter and place under the hot grill (broiler). Turn once to ensure even cooking. This will make the skins crisp and brown.

◇ Ham and Mushroom Filling Cook 100 g/4 oz/1 cup sliced mushrooms in 25 g/1 oz/2 tablespoons butter on full power for 3 minutes, then add 225 g/8 oz/1⅓ cups cubed, cooked ham. Scoop out the centre of the cooked potatoes and mix in the filling, seasoning to taste with salt and freshly ground pepper.

◇ Soured Cream and Chives Topping Stir 2 tablespoons snipped (chopped) chives into 150 ml/¼ pint/⅔ cup soured cream. Split open the cooked potatoes by making a cross in the top of each and spoon over the soured cream and chives.

◇ Avocado and Prawn (Shrimp) Filling Peel (pare), stone and roughly chop 1 large ripe avocado. Toss it with a little lemon juice, then mix with 100 g/4 oz/½ cup peeled cooked prawns (defrosted if frozen). Stir a little single (light) cream or natural yogurt into 6 tablespoons mayonnaise to thin it slightly. Season to taste and use to dress the prawn and avocado mixture. Divide the filling between the cooked potatoes and sprinkle with a little chopped parsley.

PENNE WITH GREEN VEGETABLES

◇ SERVES 4 ◇

225 g/8 oz penne (pasta quills)
1.15 litres/2 pints/5 cups boiling water
2 tablespoons vegetable oil
225 g/8 oz broccoli
100 g/4 oz French (green or snap) beans
2 courgettes (zucchini)
75 g/3 oz/6 tablespoons butter
50 g/2 oz/⅓ cup grated Parmesan cheese
salt and freshly ground black pepper

Place the pasta in a large ovenproof bowl, pour in the water and oil, then cover with cling film (plastic wrap), leaving a small gap for the steam to escape. Cook on full power for 9 minutes, stirring once during cooking. Leave to stand for a further 10 minutes then drain.

Meanwhile, divide the broccoli into small florets, cutting any large pieces of stalk into dice. Top, tail and halve the French beans and slice the courgettes. Place all the vegetables in a bowl with 2 tablespoons water, cover and cook for 5 minutes. Drain well, then stir in small knobs of butter, the cheese, drained pasta and seasoning. Cook for 3 minutes to heat through. Serve immediately.

PUDDINGS AND DESSERTS

CRÈME CARAMEL

◇ SERVES 4 ◇

• CARAMEL •

6 tablespoons water

100 g/4 oz/½ cup sugar

• CUSTARD •

3 eggs

25 g/1 oz/2 tablespoons sugar

350 ml/12 fl oz/1½ cups milk

First prepare the caramel by placing the water and sugar in an ovenproof jug (pitcher); stir well. Cook on full power for 10 to 12 minutes until golden. Do not allow the syrup to become too brown as it will continue to cook after you have removed it from the oven. Pour quickly into an 18-cm/7-in soufflé dish, then allow to cool and harden.

Whisk (beat) the eggs with the sugar until well blended. Place the milk in a heatproof, glass jug (pitcher) and cook for 4 minutes. Gradually add to the egg mixture, blending well. Pour or strain the mixture over the caramel. Cover and stand in a shallow dish. Pour enough hot water into the outer dish to come half-way up the sides of the soufflé dish. Cook for 3 to 4 minutes, giving the dish a turn once, until lightly set. Chill thoroughly.

To serve, invert the crème caramel on to a serving dish.

UPSIDE-DOWN CHOCOLATE PUDDING

◇ SERVES 4 ◇

- 25 g/1 oz/2 tablespoons butter
- 25 g/1 oz/$\frac{2}{3}$ cup soft (light) brown sugar
- 1 (411-g/14$\frac{1}{2}$-oz) can/2 cups canned pear halves, drained
- 25 g/1 oz/3 tablespoons chopped nuts

• TOPPING •

- 50 g/2 oz/4 tablespoons soft margarine
- 50 g/2 oz/$\frac{1}{4}$ cup caster sugar
- 40 g/1$\frac{1}{2}$ oz/$\frac{1}{3}$ cup plain flour
- 15 g/$\frac{1}{2}$ oz/2 tablespoons cocoa
- $\frac{1}{2}$ teaspoon baking powder
- 1 egg
- 1 tablespoon water

Place the butter and brown sugar in an 18-cm/7-in soufflé dish and cook on full power for 1 minute. Stir to mix the butter and sugar together. Arrange the pears, rounded side down, in the base of the dish and sprinkle the nuts between them.

Put all the topping ingredients into a bowl and beat together until well mixed. Spoon the mixture over the fruit, cover with a sheet of absorbent kitchen paper and cook on full power for 6 minutes. Allow to stand for 2 minutes then turn out on to a serving dish.

SERVING SUGGESTION

Serve with whipped cream, strained yogurt or pouring custard. A chocolate custard would be appropriate and you'll find a recipe for this on page 64. Alternatively, you might like to thicken the pear juices with a little cornflour (cornstarch) or arrowroot and serve them as a sauce.

TIPSY CAKE

◇ SERVES 4–6 ◇

Variations on the tipsy theme can be made by soaking the sponge in brandy-flavoured coffee syrup or by making a chocolate sponge and soaking it in a rum-flavoured sugar syrup.

75 g/3 oz/¾ cup plain flour
75 g/3 oz/4 tablespoons sugar
75 g/3 oz/6 tablespoons soft margarine
½ teaspoon baking powder
2 eggs
175 g/6 oz/½ cup seedless raspberry jam or jelly
6 tablespoons sherry
2 tablespoons brandy
150 ml/¼ pint/⅔ cup whipping (heavy) cream

Put the flour, sugar, margarine, baking powder and eggs in a bowl and beat together until well mixed.

Base line and grease an 18-cm/7-in soufflé dish and spoon the mixture into it. Cover with a sheet of absorbent kitchen paper and cook on full power for 4 minutes. The cake should be dry on top. Turn it out on to a wire rack and remove the lining paper. Leave to cool.

When cold break the cake up into pieces and put them into a large bowl. Put the jam into a bowl and heat on full power for 1 to 1½ minutes, stirring after about 45 seconds and again at the end when the jam should be melted. Pour it over the cake pieces and stir the two together until well mixed. Pour on the sherry and brandy and continue stirring and mixing until all are well blended together. The mixture will be very moist.

Spoon the mixture into a 600-ml/1-pint/2½-cup pudding basin or bowl and put a saucer on top of it. Make sure the saucer fits inside the basin and rests on the mixture. Place a weight on top and leave in a cool place overnight.

Turn the tipsy cake out on to a serving plate. Whip the cream until thick and smooth it over the pudding. Decorate either with angelica and glacé cherries or toasted flaked almonds.

APPLE CREAM WITH BLACKBERRY SAUCE

◇ SERVES 4 ◇

You can use this recipe as a basis for other combinations of creams and sauces. For instance a raspberry cream would be lovely with a redcurrant sauce. All you have to remember is to keep the colours and flavours complementary.

- 675 g/1½ lb cooking (green) apples
- 75 g/3 oz/6 tablespoons sugar
- 6 tablespoons apple juice
- 3 teaspoons powdered gelatine
- 150 ml/¼ pint/⅔ cup single (light) cream

• BLACKBERRY SAUCE •

- 225 g/8 oz/2 cups blackberries
- 50 g/2 oz/¼ cup sugar
- 1 teaspoon cornflour (cornstarch)

Peel, core and slice the apples and place in a dish with the sugar and 6 tablespoons of the apple juice. Cover with cling film (plastic wrap), leaving a small gap for the steam to escape, and cook on full power for 7 to 9 minutes or until the apples are completely soft.

Put the remaining apple juice in a small bowl, sprinkle the gelatine over it and leave to soften for about 10 minutes, then heat on full power for 15 to 30 seconds until dissolved. Stir until completely dissolved.

Purée the apples in a blender or food processor and stir in the gelatine. Leave to cool then stir in the cream and pour the mixture into a 900-ml/1½-pint/3¾-cup ring mould. Leave to set.

To make the sauce, put the blackberries into a dish and stir in the sugar and cornflour. Cover with cling film (plastic wrap), leaving a small gap for the steam to escape, and cook on full power for 3 minutes, stirring once. The blackberries should have collapsed and the juices should be very slightly thickened by the cornflour. Set aside to cool.

Turn the apple cream out on to a dish and drizzle a little of the sauce over it. Serve the rest separately.

STUFFED PEARS IN COINTREAU SAUCE

◇ SERVES 6 ◇

175 g/6 oz/$\frac{3}{4}$ cup sugar
300 ml/$\frac{1}{2}$ pint/1$\frac{1}{4}$ cups water
grated rind and juice of 1 orange
juice of 1 lemon
6 large, ripe pears
1–2 tablespoons Cointreau

• FILLING •

75 g/3 oz/$\frac{1}{2}$ cup ground almonds
50 g/2 oz/$\frac{1}{2}$ cup icing (confectioners') sugar
25 g/1 oz/2 tablespoons butter, softened
grated rind and juice of 1 orange

Place the sugar, water and orange rind in a large soufflé dish and cook on full power for 5 minutes. Stir to dissolve the sugar and cook for a further 3 minutes. Stir in the orange juice.

Meanwhile, make the filling by mixing together the almonds, sugar, butter and grated rind of the orange. Bind with a little orange juice, if necessary.

Have ready a bowl of water to which you have added half the lemon juice. As you peel and core the pears put them into the water. When all are prepared take out one at a time and fill with the stuffing. Place them in the orange syrup, upright or on their sides. Spoon the syrup over each one as you put it in the dish. Cover with cling film (plastic wrap), leaving a small gap for the steam to escape, and cook for 5 minutes, rearrange and cook for a further 3 minutes, until tender.

Transfer the pears to a serving dish. Cook the juices, uncovered, for 5 minutes to reduce a little. Stir in the remaining lemon juice together with the Cointreau. Pour over the pears. Serve hot or cold.

NUTTY GOOSEBERRY PUDDING

◇ SERVES 4 ◇

The crunchy layers of crumbs and nuts are a pleasing contrast to the smooth purée. This recipe is easily adapted to other fruit and nut combinations such as apricots and almonds; apples and walnuts.

- 675 g/1½ lb gooseberries
- 100–175 g/4–6 oz/½–¾ cup sugar
- 25 g/1 oz/2 tablespoons butter
- 50 g/2 oz/⅔ cup soft brown breadcrumbs
- 25 g/1 oz/¼ cup toasted hazelnuts, chopped
- 25 g/1 oz/2 tablespoons demerara sugar

Turn the gooseberries into an ovenproof dish with 2 tablespoons water, cover with cling film (plastic wrap), leaving a small gap for the steam to escape, and cook on full power for 8 to 10 minutes, stirring once. Purée in a food processor or a blender then rub through a sieve. Sweeten with sugar to taste, stirring it into the warm purée until dissolved. Set aside to cool.

Put the butter in a bowl and melt on full power for 45 seconds. Stir in the breadcrumbs and cook, uncovered, for 1½ to 2 minutes until they feel dry. Spread on absorbent kitchen paper to cool. Mix the nuts, sugar and breadcrumbs together.

Layer the breadcrumb mixture and cold purée into a 600-ml/1-pint/2½-cup glass dish starting with gooseberries and ending with crumbs – two layers of each. If preferred, layer into individual dishes. Serve chilled with thick yogurt or cream.

RHUBARB AND ORANGE CHEESECAKE

◇ SERVES 6 ◇

- 75 g/3 oz/6 tablespoons butter
- 175 g/6 oz digestive biscuits/1 cup graham crackers, crushed
- 225 g/8 oz prepared rhubarb
- grated rind and juice of 1 small orange
- 50 g/2 oz/¼ cup sugar
- 3 teaspoons powdered gelatine
- 175 g/6 oz/1 cup cream cheese
- 2 eggs, separated
- 1 (150-g/5.3-oz) carton/⅔ cup rhubarb yogurt

• TO DECORATE (OPTIONAL) •

- whipped cream
- grated orange rind

Put the butter into an ovenproof bowl and melt on full power for 1 to 1½ minutes. Stir in the crushed biscuits and press into the greased base of a 20-cm/8-in loose-bottomed tin (spring mold).

Cut the rhubarb into small pieces and put in a dish with the orange rind and sugar. Cover with cling film (plastic wrap), leaving a small gap for the steam to escape, and cook for 4 minutes, stirring once. Set aside to cool.

Put the orange juice into a cup, sprinkle over the gelatine. Leave to soak for a few minutes, then melt on full power for 15 to 30 seconds. Stir until dissolved completely.

Beat the cream cheese and egg yolks together. Mix in the cooled rhubarb and juices, yogurt and gelatine. Whisk (beat) the egg whites until stiff and fold through the cream cheese mixture. Pour on to the biscuit base and chill until firm.

If liked, decorate with rosettes of whipped (beaten) cream and a little grated orange rind.

PINEAPPLE RICE BRULÉE

◇ SERVES 4 ◇

- 50 g/2 oz/¼ cup pudding (short-grain) rice
- 25 g/1 oz/2 tablespoons sugar
- 600 ml/1 pint/2½ cups milk
- 4 tablespoons double (heavy) cream
- 1 (227-g/8-oz) can/1 cup canned pineapple chunks or pieces
- 6 tablespoons caster (superfine) sugar

Put the rice, sugar and milk into a large ovenproof bowl, cover with cling film (plastic wrap), leaving a small gap for the steam to escape, and cook on full power for 8 to 10 minutes until boiling. Stir well, re-cover and cook on low power (30%) for 30 to 35 minutes, stirring every 10 minutes. Leave until cold.

Whip (beat) the cream and fold it into the rice. Drain the pineapple and fold the pieces into the rice. Turn into a soufflé dish of about 600 ml/1 pint/2½ cup capacity, which it should fill to within about 5 mm/¼ in of the top. Spoon the sugar all over the surface to cover the rice completely. Put under a hot grill (broiler) until melted and golden brown, turning it as necessary to ensure the sugar melts evenly. Leave to harden and serve chilled.

BANANA MOUSSE

◇ SERVES 4–6 ◇

2 tablespoons water
2 teaspoons powdered gelatine
3 large bananas (about 450 g/1 lb)
25 g/1 oz/2 tablespoons sugar
1 tablespoon lemon juice
2–3 tablespoons rum (optional)
150 ml/¼ pint/⅔ cup double (heavy) cream

• TO SERVE •

grated chocolate or toasted flaked almonds

Put the water into a small ovenproof dish, sprinkle over the gelatine and leave to soak, then heat for 15 to 30 seconds on full power and stir to dissolve.

Mash the bananas and stir in the sugar and lemon juice. Mix in the gelatine and the rum, if used. Lightly whip the cream and fold it through the banana mixture. Spoon into four or six ramekin dishes (custard cups) and leave to set.

Serve sprinkled with grated chocolate or toasted flaked almonds.

CHOCOLATE MINT MOUSSE

◇ SERVES 4 ◇

2 (50-g/2-oz) chocolate bars containing
peppermint sugar crisp
3 eggs, separated

Break the chocolate into an ovenproof bowl and heat on full power for 2 to 2½ minutes until melted. Stir the mixture and blend in the egg yolks.

Whisk (beat) the egg whites until stiff and fold a spoonful into the chocolate mixture to soften it. Then lightly fold in the remaining egg whites. Spoon into four small wine glasses. Chill until set. These are rich and best served without cream.

HAZELNUT SPONGE WITH CHOCOLATE SAUCE

◇ SERVES 6 ◇

- 75 g/3 oz/$\frac{1}{2}$ cup toasted hazelnuts
- 100 g/4 oz/$\frac{1}{2}$ cup butter or margarine
- 100 g/4 oz/$\frac{1}{2}$ cup caster (superfine) sugar
- 2 eggs
- 100 g/4 oz self-raising flour
- 50 g/2 oz plain (semi-sweet) chocolate chips or chopped chocolate
- 1 quantity Chocolate Sauce (page 182)

Roughly chop one third of the hazelnuts and sprinkle over the base of a buttered 1.15-litre/2-pint/2$\frac{1}{2}$-pint pudding basin or deep ovenproof bowl. Coarsely grind the remaining nuts.

Place the butter or margarine, sugar, eggs and flour in a mixing bowl and beat thoroughly until pale, soft and light in colour. Fold in the ground nuts and chocolate chips. Spoon the sponge mixture over the chopped nuts and level the surface. Cook on full power for 5 minutes turning once during cooking. Leave the sponge to stand in the basin or bowl for 5 minutes before turning out. Serve with the chocolate sauce.

BREAD SAUCE

◇ MAKES 300 ML / ½ PINT / 1¼ CUPS ◇

- 1 small onion, studded with 6 cloves
- 300 ml/½ pint/1¼ cups milk
- 75 g/3 oz/1 cup fresh breadcrumbs
- 25 g/1 oz/2 tablespoons butter
- salt and freshly ground pepper

Place the onion and the milk in a 600-ml/1-pint/2½-cup measuring jug (pitcher) and cook on full power for 4 minutes. Stand for 30 minutes. Remove the onion and stir in the breadcrumbs, butter and seasoning. Reheat in the microwave for 1 to 2 minutes before serving.

SERVING SUGGESTION

Bread sauce is a traditional accompaniment to roast chicken and turkey or game. When prepared in the microwave, the onion gives the sauce a particularly good flavour without leaving it to stand for a long time to infuse.

WHITE SAUCE

◇ MAKES 300 ML / ½ PINT / 1¼ CUPS ◇

25 g/1 oz/2 tablespoons butter
25 g/1 oz/4 tablespoons flour
300 ml/½ pint/1¼ cups milk
salt and freshly ground pepper

Melt the butter in a glass measuring jug (pitcher) in the microwave on full power for 1 minute. Stir in the flour until well mixed then pour in the milk and stir well. Cook in the microwave for 4 minutes, stirring after every minute to prevent lumps forming. Season to taste.

• VARIATIONS •

◇ Anchovy Sauce Add 1–2 teaspoons anchovy essence and a squeeze of lemon juice to the cooked sauce. Serve with fish.

◇ Cheese Sauce Stir 50 g/2 oz/½ cup grated cheese into the cooked sauce. Serve with poultry, ham and vegetables.

◇ Egg Sauce Finely chop 2 hard-boiled eggs and add to the sauce. Serve with fish.

◇ Mushroom Sauce Stir about 50 g/2 oz/½ cup sliced cooked mushrooms and a dash of Worcestershire sauce into the cooked sauce. Serve with fish and poultry.

◇ Lemon Sauce Stir the juice and rind of ½ lemon into the cooked sauce. Serve with fish and poultry.

◇ Parsley Sauce Stir 1–2 tablespoons chopped parsley into the cooked sauce. Serve with bacon and fish.

ONION SAUCE

◇ MAKES 300 ML / ½ PINT / 1¼ CUPS ◇

- 25 g/1 oz/2 tablespoons butter
- 1 large onion, thinly sliced
- 25 g/1 oz/4 tablespoons flour
- 300 ml/½ pint/1¼ cups milk
- salt and freshly ground pepper

Place the butter and onion slices in a 1-litre/2-pint/2½-pint ovenproof bowl and cook in the microwave on full power for 5 minutes, stirring twice during cooking. Stir in the flour, then add the milk and mix well. Return to the microwave for 3 minutes, stirring once. Season to taste. Onion sauce is delicious with lamb dishes.

HOLLANDAISE SAUCE

◇ MAKES ABOUT 300 ML / ½ PINT / 1¼ CUPS ◇

- 2 tablespoons lemon juice
- 3 egg yolks
- salt and white pepper
- 100 g/4 oz/½ cup butter

Put the lemon juice and egg yolks into an ovenproof bowl with a seasoning of salt and white pepper and whisk together.

Put the butter, cut into pieces, in a bowl and melt on full power for 1 to 1½ minutes. Pour the butter slowly on to the egg mixture whisking (beating) all the time.

Cook the mixture for 45 seconds, whisking well every 15 seconds until thick. It may need a few more seconds but take care not to overheat or it will curdle. The mixture should be warm not hot.

Serve warm or cold with fish and vegetables.

TOMATO SAUCE

◇ MAKES ABOUT 450 ML / ¾ PINT / 2 CUPS ◇

- 1 tablespoon oil
- 1 onion, finely chopped
- 1 clove garlic, crushed
- 1 (397-g/14-oz) can/2 cups canned chopped tomatoes
- 2 tablespoons concentrated tomato purée
- 1 teaspoon chopped fresh basil
- 1 teaspoon sugar
- salt and freshly ground pepper

Place the oil, onion and garlic in an ovenproof bowl, cover with cling film (plastic wrap), leaving a small gap for the steam to escape, and cook on full power for 2 minutes. Stir in the remaining ingredients and cook for 3 minutes. Stir and cook for a further 3 minutes. Check the seasoning before using.

Rub it through a sieve if you prefer a smooth sauce.

SERVING SUGGESTION

A simple tomato sauce can be served with fish, poultry or meat dishes. It can also be used to coat vegetables, for example courgettes, aubergines or cauliflower, or it can be served with cooked pasta to make a light supper dish. A sprinkling of Parmesan cheese and chopped parsley completes the dish.

BOLOGNESE SAUCE

◇ SERVES 4 ◇

- 1 tablespoon oil
- 1 onion, finely chopped
- 1 carrot, finely chopped
- 2 rashers (slices) streaky (Canadian) bacon, chopped
- 350 g/12 oz minced or ground beef
- 100 g/4 oz chicken livers, chopped
- 1 (227-g/8-oz) can/1 cup canned tomatoes
- 1 tablespoon concentrated tomato purée
- 4 tablespoons white wine or stock
- salt and pepper

Put the oil, onion, carrot and bacon into a bowl, cover with cling film (plastic wrap), leaving a small gap for the steam to escape, and cook on full power for 4 minutes. Stir in the beef, breaking down any lumps. Cover and cook for 4 minutes, stirring once. Stir in the chicken livers, tomatoes, breaking them up well, tomato purée and wine or stock. Season with salt and freshly ground pepper. Cover and cook for 5 minutes, stirring once. Check the seasoning and serve with pasta.

SERVING SUGGESTION

Try serving bolognese sauce in baked potatoes or with some cooked rice to make a simple meal. The sauce can be layered up with lasagne, then topped with cheese sauce and reheated. This sauce can also be used to fill cooked pancakes (prepare these conventionally).

CHOCOLATE SAUCE

◇ SERVES 4 ◇

- 15 g/½ oz/2 tablespoons cornflour (cornstarch)
- 25 g/1 oz/2 tablespoons soft (light) brown sugar
- 300 ml/½ pint/1¼ cups milk
- 50 g/2 oz plain (semi-sweet) chocolate
- 25 g/1 oz/2 tablespoons butter

In a large ovenproof bowl, mix together the cornflour and sugar. Gradually stir in the milk. Break the chocolate into small pieces and add to the bowl. Cook on full power for 3½ minutes, stirring twice during cooking. Whisk (beat) in the butter at the end of the cooking time. Serve immediately.

RICH CHOCOLATE SAUCE

◇ MAKES 300 ML / ½ PINT / 1¼ CUPS ◇

A rich chocolate sauce to serve hot with ice cream or cool over profiteroles. Store in the refrigerator and reheat when needed.

- 175 g/6 oz plain (semi-sweet) chocolate
- 50 g/2 oz/¼ cup soft (light) brown sugar
- 4 tablespoons water
- 50 g/2 oz/4 tablespoons butter

Put the chocolate, brown sugar and water in an ovenproof bowl and melt on full power for 2 minutes. Stir.

Cut the butter into small cubes and stir a few at a time into the chocolate, adding more as the previous pieces melt. If necessary, return to microwave towards the end and heat for 15 seconds to soften the last pieces of butter.

The butter must not oil but just soften sufficiently to blend into the chocolate.

BANANA AND BUTTERSCOTCH SAUCE

◇ SERVES 4 ◇

50 g/2 oz/$\frac{1}{4}$ cup butter
100 g/4 oz/$\frac{1}{2}$ cup soft (light) brown sugar
3 tablespoons single (light) cream
1 large banana

Put the butter and sugar into an ovenproof bowl, cover with cling film (plastic wrap), leaving a small gap for the steam to escape, and cook on full power for 2 minutes. Stir well to amalgamate the sugar and butter and cook for another 30 to 60 seconds until the mixture boils and thickens. Stir in the cream, mixing well.

Cut the banana into small chunks and stir it into the sauce. Reheat for 1 minute and spoon over vanilla ice cream.

FRUIT SAUCE

◇ MAKES 600 ML / 1 PINT / $2\frac{1}{2}$ CUPS ◇

100 g/4 oz/$\frac{3}{4}$ cup no-need-to-soak apricots
300 ml/$\frac{1}{2}$ pint/$1\frac{1}{4}$ cups water
50 g/2 oz/$\frac{1}{4}$ cup sugar
1 (376-g/13.3-oz) can/1 cup
canned crushed pineapple

Put apricots into a dish with the water, cover with cling film (plastic wrap), leaving a small gap for the steam to escape, and cook on full power for 10 minutes. Stir in sugar and crushed pineapple and cook for a further 3 minutes. Turn into a food processor or blender and purée the fruits. The mixture will not be completely smooth.

Serve hot with sponge pudding or cold with ice cream.

PRESERVES AND SWEETS

GREEN TOMATO CHUTNEY

◇ MAKES ABOUT 675 G / 1½ LB ◇

- 1 medium onion, finely chopped
- 300 ml/½ pint/1¼ cups vinegar
- 450 g/1 lb green tomatoes, peeled and chopped
- 2 apples, peeled, cored and chopped
- ½ teaspoon mustard powder
- pinch of ground ginger
- pinch of salt
- 100 g/4 oz/⅔ cup sultanas
- 100 g/4 oz/⅔ cup caster (superfine) sugar

Place the chopped onion in a 600-ml/1-pint/2½-cup measuring jug (pitcher) with half the vinegar. Cover with cling film (plastic wrap) and cook on full power for 5 minutes. Transfer to a large mixing bowl and add the tomatoes, apple, mustard powder, ginger, salt and sultanas. Cover and cook in the microwave for 10 minutes, stirring frequently.

Stir in the sugar and the remaining vinegar. Return to the microwave and cook for a further 15 minutes, stirring once during cooking.

Bottle in sterilized jars (see page 77), seal and label.

DRIED FRUIT CHUTNEY

◇ MAKES 1.25–1.5 KG / 2½–3 LBS ◇

900 g/2 lbs/6 cups dried fruit (dates, raisins, apricots, sultanas)
350 g/12 oz/1½ cups (light) brown sugar
1 medium onion, finely chopped
2 cloves garlic, crushed
2 teaspoons ground mixed spice
450 ml/¾ pint/2 cups cider vinegar

Chop the fruit roughly and put all the ingredients in a large ovenproof bowl. Cover with cling film (plastic wrap), leaving a small gap for the steam to escape, and cook on full power for 20 minutes. Stir and cook, uncovered, for another 10 minutes, or until the mixture is thick, stirring frequently.

Pot and cover in the usual way.

STRAWBERRY CONSERVE

◇ MAKES ABOUT 675 G / 1½ LB ◇

450 g/1 lb small strawberries
450 g/1 lb/2 cups sugar
4 tablespoons lemon juice

Hull the strawberries. Place them in a large bowl with the sugar and lemon juice. Toss the fruit lightly until it is thoroughly coated with the sugar. Cover and stand overnight.

The following day uncover the soaked fruit and cook on full power for 16 minutes, stirring twice during the first 5 minutes. Transfer the conserve, which will be syrupy not firmly set, to warmed pots and cover these immediately with waxed discs and airtight lids.

LEMON CURD

◇ MAKES JUST OVER 450 G / 1 LB ◇

100 g/4 oz/½ cup unsalted (sweet) butter
2 large or 3 small lemons
225 g/8 oz/1 cup caster (superfine) sugar
3 eggs, beaten

Put the butter in an ovenproof bowl and melt on full power for 1 to 1½ minutes. Grate the rinds and squeeze the juice from the lemons.

Stir the sugar, lemon rind and juice into the melted butter. Strain and stir in the eggs. Cook, uncovered, for 4½ to 5 minutes, stirring after each minute for 4 minutes, then check after a further 30 seconds. If it coats the back of the spoon, it is ready. It will thicken further on cooling.

Pour into small sterilized jars (see page 77) and seal while hot.

ORANGE CURD

◇ MAKES JUST OVER 450 G / 1 LB ◇

100 g/4 oz/½ cup unsalted (sweet) butter
175 g/6 oz/¾ cup caster (superfine) sugar
grated rind and juice of 2 oranges
4 tablespoons frozen orange juice concentrate, thawed
3 eggs, beaten

Put the butter in an ovenproof bowl and melt on full power for 1 to 1½ minutes.

Stir the sugar, orange rind and juice and the orange juice concentrate into the melted butter. Strain and stir in the eggs. Cook, uncovered, for 4½ to 5 minutes, stirring after each minute for 4 minutes, then checking after a further 30 seconds. If it coats the back of the spoon, it is ready. It will thicken further on cooling.

Pour into small sterilized jars (see page 77) and seal while hot.

THREE FRUITS MARMALADE

◇ MAKES ABOUT 1.25 KG / 2½ LB ◇

675 g/1½ lb citrus fruits (1 large grapefruit, 1 large lemon and 2 oranges)
600 ml/1 pint/2½ cups water
450–675 g/1–1½ lbs/2–3 cups sugar

Wash the fruit and peel it thinly, avoiding the pith. With a sharp knife, cut the peel into narrow strips. Cut the fruit in half and squeeze out the juice. Pour it into a large ovenproof, glass bowl with the water, the peel and the pips and pith tied in a muslin or cloth bag. Cover with cling film (plastic wrap) and cook for 17 to 20 minutes until the peel is tender. Remove the pith and pips. Measure the juice and allow 450 g/1 lb/2 cups sugar to each 600 ml/1 pint/2½ cups of juice. Return the juice and sugar to the bowl, stir well and cook on full power for 20 minutes, or until setting point is reached. Cool and pot in the usual way.

CHOCOLATE HAZELNUT FUDGE

◇ MAKES ABOUT 800 G / 1¾ LBS ◇

450 g/1 lb/3⅓ cup icing (confectioners') sugar
50 g/2 oz/⅓ cup (unsweetened) cocoa powder or
175 g/6 oz plain (bitter) chocolate
100 g/4 oz/½ cup butter
4 tablespoons milk
75 g/3 oz/½ cup toasted hazelnuts

Sift the icing sugar into a large bowl with the cocoa powder, if using. Place the butter, milk and chocolate, if used, into a jug (pitcher) and melt on full power for 1 to 2 minutes.

Pour it on to the sugar, stirring, then beat well until thick and creamy. Stir in the hazelnuts and spoon into an 18-cm/7-in square cake tin (pan), lightly greased. Leave to set and cut into squares.

ORANGE FUDGE

◇ MAKES ABOUT 350 G / 12 OZ ◇

- 225 g/8 oz/1 cup sugar
- 150 ml/¼ pint/⅔ cup milk
- 50 g/2 oz/¼ cup butter or margarine
- grated rind of 1 orange
- 1 teaspoon orange flower water (optional)

Lightly grease a 12-cm/5-in square tin (pan) or dish. Place the sugar, milk and butter or margarine in a large ovenproof bowl. Cook on full power for 11 minutes, stirring after 2 minutes, then every 30 seconds during the last 3 minutes. Add the orange rind and orange flower water, if using, then beat the mixture well until it begins to thicken and becomes slightly 'grainy'. Pour into the prepared tin (pan) or dish. When almost set cut into squares.

CRÈME DE MENTHE DELIGHT

◇ MAKES ABOUT 350 G / 12 OZ ◇

- 225 g/8 oz/1 cup granulated sugar
- 150 ml/¼ pint/⅔ cup water
- 3 teaspoons powdered gelatine
- 1 tablespoon crème de menthe
- generous pinch of cream of tartar
- 25 g/1 oz/¼ cup icing (confectioners') sugar, sifted

Place the granulated sugar and all but 3 tablespoons of the water in a large ovenproof bowl. Cook on full power for 3 minutes, stirring twice to dissolve the sugar.

Sprinkle the gelatine over the remaining water and leave for 1 to 2 minutes to become spongy. Cook for 30 seconds, then stir until the gelatine is dissolved. Stir the gelatine mixture into the sugar syrup and cook for 8 minutes, stirring twice during cooking. Quickly stir in the liqueur and cream of tartar, then pour into a damp 12-cm/5-in square tin (pan). Allow to set. Cut into squares with scissors and roll in icing sugar.

DIPPED BRANDY TRUFFLES

◇ MAKES ABOUT 15 ◇

- 100 g/4 oz plain (bitter) chocolate
- 25 g/1 oz/2 tablespoons butter
- 1 egg yolk
- 2 teaspoons brandy
- 2 teaspoons cream
- 40 g/1½ oz/½ cup finely ground cake crumbs

• TO FINISH •

- 100 g/4 oz white chocolate

Put the chocolate and butter in a bowl and melt on full power for 1 to 2 minutes. Stir in the egg yolk, then the brandy and cream. Finally stir in the cake crumbs until well mixed and thick. Cover and refrigerate until firm.

Shape the mixture into small balls and open freeze until quite firm.

Put the white chocolate in a small ovenproof bowl and melt for 1 to 2 minutes.

Put one truffle at a time in the chocolate, turning it with a teaspoon or fork to coat it thinly. Lift on to a sheet of greaseproof (waxed) paper or foil to set. The chocolate will set almost immediately on the cold truffle. Store in the refrigerator.

INDEX